Les Dawson was one of Britain's finest and best-loved comedians. He wrote twelve books, which range from comic novels and joke books to travel and fiction.

Until his sudden death in June, 1993, he lived in Lytham St Annes, Lancashire, with his wife Tracy. Between them they had five children from previous marriages and in 1992, to their delight, Tracy gave birth to a baby daughter.

No Tears for the Clown

An Autobiography

LES DAWSON

A *Warner* Book

First published in Great Britain in 1992 by Robson Books Ltd
This edition published by Warner Books in 1993

A CIP catalogue record for this book
is available from the British Library.

ISBN 0 7515 0487 4

Printed in England by Clays Ltd, St Ives plc

Warner Books
A Division of
Little, Brown and Company (UK) Limited
165 Great Dover Street
London SE1 4YA

I dedicate this book to Poo, for chasing away the shadows and letting me live again; and to all our friends who encouraged our love.

A note to the reader

I have quite purposely omitted to include dates pertaining to events because I didn't want my autobiography to read like a diary. I wanted to convey an impression of my life rather than a blow by blow account; I felt that the reader and I should relive its ups and downs in a series of word pictures.

I lived with the knowledge that a loved one was going to die, and when death took the loved one away from me, I saw my life as an arid stretch of loneliness and empty days. Instead, somehow, love came into my existence and I hope to pass on the joy that was wrought in my soul. So I beg of you, look upon this little offering as a sort of good-natured ramble through some passionate years.

It may very well be that I have not described the things that happened in strict chronological order; it doesn't matter: the happenings were experienced, and that is what it is all about is it not?

Les Dawson

No Tears for the Clown

Prelude

I genuinely believed that when my autobiography, *A Clown Too Many*, was published in the mid nineteen eighties, it would be the only book about my life, but so many things have happened since then that people have urged me to write another volume chronicling events that have been both comic and tragic.

I was very moved by the sentiments expressed by so many folk who had read *A Clown Too Many*, and it was rewarding for me to realise that the public in general appreciated the fact that I was simply an ordinary little chap who happened to be an entertainer, and enjoyed being just that.

Like so many others, I have discovered that the older I get, the less I know. I don't know why there is so much pain and heartache in our lives.... Like many others I question the existence of God, then I look at the vast cathedral of a night sky and I have to admit to a grudging acknowledgement of a power far greater than anything Man has created. Does Mankind possess twin souls? One that caters to a dark, cruel, demonic nature, and one that is nourished on compassion and kindness?

My own sojourn in this vale of tears only strengthens my belief in love and friendship as spiritual bedfellows.... To win the love of a child, to earn the enthusiastic approbation of an audience that is warm and friendly and holds you in a cocoon of intimacy – these are to experience a great joy. To love a woman and to be loved by her in return, makes a man rich beyond the dreams of avarice. These are old concepts, I know, but the truth of them becomes very clear when an individual is faced with adversity.

It is the unseen things that cause humanity the most pain: the insincerity of politics; the cant of religious bigotry and plain human jealousy that begins in the philosophy of desire.

Since we humans first plodded out from the primordial swamps and stood upright to pee, we have done our damnedest to make life difficult for ourselves – and that statement doesn't include trying to kill each other off on a wholesale basis. It speaks well, therefore, for the human spirit, that we have not only managed to survive, but have even found the ability to laugh at ourselves in spite of our self-inflicted wounds. Our society today is a most cynical one. It's my honest belief that if Christ came amongst us tomorrow, he'd be put on television and be offered a job as a game-show host. I fear that once we lose that ability to laugh at ourselves we are on a slippery slope indeed.

In this, the second volume of my autobiography, I have put on paper the truth of things, and I have pulled no punches. Despite a lot of kicks, Life has been good to me, and I'd like to be around to see Part Three published. I suppose a fitting epitaph for my last resting place would read: 'Well, what was life but a theme for quips?'

Reflections

He felt good, and the only burning necessity at that moment was to clamber out of the car after the three-hour drive through the hell of a motorway jam, and sprint into the loo to relieve a swollen bladder.

He stood before the lavatory bowl and waited for the water to cascade. It didn't, and a pain shot across his kidneys. Three times that night he attempted to relieve himself, and finally a feeble trickle roused itself into a stream and the pain subsided.

He didn't think much about it – it was probably a chill on the kidneys. He felt fit enough; capable of doing twice-nightly variety shows then drinking heavily, which he did sometimes in a stupid attempt to momentarily forget that his wife had cancer.... No, he was in fine fettle all right.

The following day he went off to play golf in a charity competition to raise money for handicapped children. He played lousily but enjoyed the game, and in the bar he drank two pints of lager with his crony, Richard Gill.

He trotted off to the gents and found he couldn't pass water and the pain came back.

He drove home and his distended abdomen made breathing difficult. The pain in his back became intolerable as the afternoon changed into the shades of early evening.

He tried a hot bath, but to no avail; by now he felt faint with the fire in his kidneys and he crawled on all fours to the downstairs telephone. His wife was asleep in her sick bed, his daughter, Julie, had gone for groceries and his other children, Stuart and Pamela, were with friends down the road.

The starched voice of the doctor's receptionist, in response to his plea for help, asked him if he could call at the surgery? He answered back angrily as the pain knifed through him.... Finally the doctor arrived. After an internal probe, he told the sufferer that his prostate gland wasn't functioning any more and there and then made arrangements for him to be taken into the Preston Hospital to have the defunct prostate removed.

Dr Bob Thompson operated – all was well: he was satisfied that the gland was not malignant. Gone now the pain, and the man felt at ease despite the catheter at his side.

Release date loomed: the man's family brought his clothes – all augured well. Suddenly he began to shiver violently and his vision faltered. A nurse ran to his side – she paled and pressed a bell for assistance – now he felt hands hoisting him on to a trolley – lights on the ceiling were flashing by in quick succession – voices clamouring – someone pushing needles into him....

He heard someone shout, 'He's got blood poisoning.' Noise, noise, more hands guiding him into a bed and more attempts to push a needle into him.

He raved and mouthed oaths; his body shook and spittle ran down the corners of his mouth.

He slept. He awoke with a burning thirst; some Samaritan wiped his cracked lips with water....

For four nights he hovered on the edge of death. It would be a long time before he forgot the events of 1985.

* * *

The doctor came and went after reassuring me that the poisons had been eliminated from my blood and that I was now starting to mend. Frankly, I felt his words lacked conviction and I wondered if he had a commission rate going with an undertaker. I looked lousy and I felt lousy and I was feeling very sorry for myself into the bargain.

The operation on my prostate gland seemingly had gone awry, and the good medics at Preston had snatched me from the waiting arms of the Grim Reaper. After four days in the intensive care unit, the healing fraternity had chortled with triumph and carted me back to the ward proper. I don't recall if I was a good patient or not, but as my friend Gilly wheeled me out of the hospital, the entire staff waved their arms vigorously – I thought this was nice until I noticed that they all had their fists clenched. I do confess to being slightly perturbed when I discovered that the braking system on the wheelchair had been tampered with, but I put that down to National Health inefficiency.

Now at last I was back home, lying in bed and making rude gestures to the rear of the disappearing doctor. At my side, Meg, my wife of twenty-five years, stirred to wakefulness and my self-pitying interlude was over, for my wife had cancer of the spine and pain was her constant companion.

I ended Book One of my autobiography, *A Clown Too Many,* with these words: 'Meg turned to me: "Look at us," she said with a wan smile. "A pair of crocks." I kissed her, held her close and said, "Sweetheart, we'll beat 'em yet." And you know something? We will.'

Brave words, but Fate had other plans.

Our elder daughter, Julie, who is a nurse, had come home from the University Hospital in Nottingham to look after her mother. Now the poor lass had two sick people to worry about. She was still a student nurse but she looked every inch a pro as she deftly cared for us – not bad for a girl of nineteen.

I felt so weak and tearful. The slightest kindness brought a lump to my throat. I looked a mess: my eyes were inside dark tunnels and I badly needed a shave. I was thin and brimming with self-pity. The hospital food had made me retch, and now all I wanted to do was sleep.

Slowly I built my health back up – much, I suspect, to the chagrin of certain tabloid reporters who had virtually camped outside the hospital waiting for the announcement that I had shuffled off the mortal coil. One enterprising hack even sent me a note after my discharge from the Preston hospital. It read quite pithily: 'You ruined my headline: "Eric Morecambe ... Tommy Cooper ... now Les Dawson: the last of the comic dinosaurs".'

Despite everything, I had to laugh! That's the sort of tacky, so-called journalism that I find offensive, and that brings British newspaper reporting into disrepute.

Julie spoiled Meg and me something awful ... but it was awfully nice! Meg's spirits were something to be admired, although it was so apparent that she was in pain.

As the weeks progressed, my weight increased and the skeletal appearance gave way to the old fat-faced clown with looks that could stop Big Ben, let alone an ordinary clock. I was getting restless as well. Meg wasn't showing any improvement whatsoever despite the fine treatment she'd received, and I needed to work again ... and fast. The Inland Revenue still want their dues; the building society still needs to be nourished, and the bills still have to be paid, because they, like the tax and the mortgage, are no respecters of illness and misfortune. Many people must think: 'What's he on about? He's all right, makes a fortune on the box.' Crap. If I was a millionaire, my friends, I wouldn't be away from home in digs knocking myself out twice daily in summer seasons and pantomimes.

It was time to take my wife to Christie's Hospital in Manchester, possibly the finest cancer unit in the world. Despite the daily parade of pain and sadness and futility, the staff there meet you with a smile, gentle reassurance and friendliness. As we waited for the specialists, we looked around at the other patients who were suffering this most dreaded of all ills. Cancer knows no class, no age group, it just destroys all in its path.

Meg's turn came and we sat down in the specialist's room. Whilst he examined my wife I made small talk with the nurse and even managed to raise a smile or two. We needed a laugh....

Two years previously, it had looked as if Meg's operation for a mastectomy had been fully successful. The surgeon who performed it at Victoria Hospital in Blackpool had been highly satisfied with the result and life seemed rosy again. But then it had happened. Six months later Meg had slipped and fallen heavily in St Anne's Square. She recovered all right from the fall, and all seemed well... we didn't know that the cancer had flared up again in her spine.

She began to have a great deal of pain down her left leg and I took her to our local GP, who packed us off to our cottage hospital in Lytham for an X-ray.

As a result of the X-ray sciatica was diagnosed, and she was treated for this complaint; then, a little while later, we were informed that the wrong X-ray had been looked at. Another eminent specialist at Christie's examined her and more X-rays were taken. Whilst awaiting these new findings I cracked gags about hospitals and Meg looked radiant and I thought smugly: 'She's going to be OK. . . .'

The receptionist took Meg off for a cup of tea whilst I went to spend a penny. On the way back I inadvertently wandered into another room, just in time to see the specialist gazing intently at Meg's X-rays. He was unaware of my presence, so had no reason to disguise the sad shake of his head or to alter the expression of futility so patently on his face. I couldn't breathe . . . I wanted to shout out to him: 'What have you seen in those damned pictures?' But of course I didn't. Instead I tiptoed out and found the room I'd been sitting in before.

I tried to focus on a magazine but my eyes were blurred with tears. I knew with a sickening certainty that the cancer had spread and that she was going to die. . . . My heart beat a maddened tattoo and my mouth was dry. I was barely aware that Meg had re-entered the room. She looked bright and happy. . . . What's that she's saying? Why is the receptionist laughing, and *why is the specialist lying*?

My head was swimming. I had to get out into the fresh air, to be amongst people who hadn't got cancer. . . . I lit up a cigarette and plunged into a trough of self-pity. Yes, I was thinking of myself, because my mind refused to believe that my partner of nearly twenty-five years was going to leave me alone. I finally pulled myself together. As I waved goodbye to the staff who came to see us off, I caught the eye of the specialist, and I knew that he was aware that the truth was now shared.

Time does indeed dull pain, as the days lengthened into weeks I began to see things more optimistically. Although Meg was now able to get about only with the aid of a stick, she seemed stronger, and life with the family resumed a nearly normal pattern. Illness can sometimes breach the family bond and create suspicion and mistrust, even to provoke a flare-up of deep-rooted enmities. Meg's illness, however, created a close feeling of unity with the children and myself and the in-laws. I was the only one who knew the absolute truth: Meg and everyone else thought it was sciatica, and so I could pretend to my heart's delight that all was well. Joke followed joke, antic pursued antic. We Dawsons acted the fool and I was the prime clown.

I made excuses for not working and lied to my back teeth to prevent Meg guessing the truth. Each morning, noon and night was a bonus; we surrounded Meg with love and affection, and I like to think that she went to God without knowing about her cancer. Our kids were wonderful, just by being themselves and treating life normally. Our pretend world became a reality. Stuart went to his karate lessons, Pamela did her homework and Julie hopped between her training hospital and home. I began to feel that all would be well.

I took Meg every week for a chat and check-up, and even the specialist appeared optimistic.

I begged my agents to get the BBC to restart the postponed series of *Blankety Blank*; apart from feeling the pinch I needed to get to grips with an audience again, and a month later I hosted the first show in the new series. It gave me the chance, although somewhat belatedly, to thank all the thousands of people who had taken the trouble to write to me whilst I had been incarcerated in hospital. Predictably, all the opening patter had to do with hospitals:

'I've just come out of hospital ... hospital, that's an abattoir with splints.'

'I had a really old-fashioned doctor, when he lanced a boil he did it on horseback.'

'They sat me on so many bedpans my bum had metal fatigue.'

'I wasn't allowed to smoke but I did until one morning I was summoned into the matron's office. Thinking quickly I shoved the packet of fags under my left armpit, and my lighter under my right armpit. The matron lifted both arms and confiscated them both. "Right, bend down," she said. "Blimey," I shouted, "don't tell me you want my chewing gum as well." '

It felt so good for an old ham like me to play an audience and pit my wits against the likes of Joe Brown, Lionel Blair, dear old Bernie Winters and Danny La Rue, not to mention the contestants who could be pretty handy with a snappy line. It kept me on my toes and it was just what I needed . . . it's a medicine in its own special way.

Also, now that money was coming in, the burden of the mounting bills was eased. I thanked God that only Pamela was still at private school: as I have mentioned, Julie was nursing and Stuart was a trainee motor mechanic, and doing well at it. He'd always been good with his hands and I looked forward to the day when he could save me some garage bills. I used to do a lot of patter about garages:

'A garage charged me ten pounds, to tow me off a motorway . . . I got my own back, all the time he was towing me I kept my brakes on.'

'A garage told me that my battery was flat. Big deal, what shape should it be?'

'I said to a garage, "Will you service my car?" They looked at it and said, "Try Lourdes." '

Meanwhile, Meg had had to start getting about on two sticks, and even that was becoming a struggle . . . all my fears came back. But once more, her dogged determination and cheerfulness allayed my anxieties, and I found myself lulled into a false security.

A convoy of cars wound its way into the golf club car park in Lytham, every one of them bringing close friends and relations to celebrate the long love of two people.

I had helped Meg into her dress. I had made sure she swallowed her pain-killers, and I had escorted her to a waiting hire-car. I had no intention of driving myself on this night: I had a date with champagne.

Meg and I stood by the clubhouse door to welcome our family and friends. As they saw Meg leaning on her sticks, they didn't show pity or concern – just an all-embracing love. Our favourite song, 'True Love', struck up and I held her in my arms. My soul melted as her green eyes looked deep into mine. 'I love you,' she whispered, and I was too choked to answer her – it was a night to hold forever in a scented memory....

Our wedding anniversary ... twenty-five years together through thick and thin, we'd known the heights and we'd known the troughs. Here we stood in the middle of the ballroom at the Green Drive Golf Club, surrounded by our friends and family.... I still see Meg to this day, dancing with me and taking every step with those amazing sticks.

I'd drunk too much, and smoked too much, and Meg cocked an eye at me: 'Your chest sounds like a foot pump,' she said. 'You'd better start looking after yourself.' She telling me – and knowing what I did ... I held her close so that she couldn't see the tears spring to my eyes.... The night was a magical one and we saw dawn flush the sky.

At one of Meg's weekly check-ups at Christie's, when it had become very apparent that her sticks were becoming useless, the specialist suggested after a scan of her lower limbs that she should go into a wheelchair.

The atmosphere in the office was one of sickening realisations: for Meg, that soon she would be dependent upon such a contraption to get around, and for me, that her condition was worsening by the day.

The children still didn't suspect anything. Julie would have done, had she been at home, but fortunately I had told her to return to Nottingham to resume her nursing career.

The wheelchair arrived and Meg sat looking at it. 'Just how bad am I?' she asked me in a low voice.

I lied to my back teeth. 'Well, obviously it isn't good, darling, but the specialist says that being in the chair will take the weight off your feet and give your legs a chance to get stronger with the radium treatment.'

Her next words shook me – she had never mentioned the word cancer before. She held my gaze. 'Has the cancer spread a lot?' she said quietly.

I wanted to shriek out: *'Yes, it's all over your body and God won't make you better and I'm helpless to do any sodding thing and I love you.'* What I did say was: 'Not a lot, angel, it's in your lower back ... that's why your legs are bad. Christie's are very happy the way the cancer is being contained, and the treatment might well help to fuse the bones more solidly and eventually get you back on your feet.... Until then, my girl, get in that chair.'

She smiled at me and kissed me. She seemed satisfied with my lies and dutifully sat in the wheelchair and started playing about with the controls. Back and forth she went, pressing the controls and roaring with delight as she grew confident with her new toy. In those early days, we had so much simple fun with the kids and Meg chasing about in her chair.... So much fun to cloak the tragedy of it all.

I was drinking somewhat heavily but it didn't ease the pain. I drank in a hotel called the St Ives. I liked the bar there and I could chat with other showbiz people who frequented the place and try to forget about my private woes for an hour. I always remember the beautiful girl behind the bar; her name was Tracy and her smile always made me feel good. She really was a stunner, and all the male customers would try to flirt with her. The hours I spent in that place helped me to find the strength to face whatever was to be.

I cooked the meals and the children attempted to swallow the mess. Mercifully, on her good days, Meg would do the cooking and thus save us the trouble of an ulcer, and a lady came in to clean the house up, so life went on. Meg was still able to walk a few yards; she could leave the wheelchair at the foot of the stairs and walk up to our bedroom, but even that was getting more and more difficult.

I knew the time had come to suggest bringing her bed downstairs – but how to do so without arousing her fears?

I was coming to the close of the third series of *Blankety Blank*, which had been going very well in the ratings, but because of Meg's condition I didn't stay in London. The BBC allowed me a limousine to take me to the studio and then, after taping the programme, run me back to the north. It was tiring and I'm not an enthusiastic traveller at the best of times. I hate traffic jams and I hate delays at airports – I particularly hate the constant searches, which always make me feel soiled somehow.

At Heathrow once, a customs official with a face like an open grave gloomily started to rummage through my suitcase. Purely for comic relief I whispered to him, 'If you let me through I'll split half the packets of hashish with you and I'll throw in some illegal Tunisian corduroy condoms.'

I thought he'd laugh. He didn't, and I was trotted off to a room and strip-searched.

Despite my problems with travelling, at least with Meg the frustrations had always been tempered with laughter. Her sense of humour brightened the most idiotic situations. I can see her now in my mind's eye, choking back the laughter at the sight of her portly spouse and a randy camel – it was on a family holiday in Egypt, and we had just visited the Pyramids. I mounted a camel which then tried to mount me – and not for sightseeing either, I might add. Upon realising that it was not going to have its way with me, the confounded flea-ridden animal got fed up trying and sat on my head instead. The family fell about and a Canadian tourist asked me to smile from under the camel's bum as he fiddled with his camera.

Meg had many occasions to laugh. Some years ago I took the family on a cruise to the West Indies. We loaded so much luggage into the taxi, one of the springs went. We reached Manchester Airport and the police phoned to say that our burglar alarm had gone off and the property was now surrounded by alert constabulary. Ten minutes later, I received another phone call, this time from a neighbour, who kindly informed us that the police had gone having found no evidence of a prowler, but that she had spotted an elderly man with a bulging bag creeping through to the rear of the premises, and she had phoned the police and they had apprehended the old chap.

Throughout this call, my son had been tugging my trousers, and at the finish I cuffed his ears soundly. As he rubbed his appendages, he shouted, 'That man isn't a burglar, it's Uncle Cyril – he's going to put that wooden frame up for you today!' Eventually I got through to our local cop shop and spoke to the sergeant. He wasn't very pleased with me, and poor Cyril was locked in a cell. They let me speak to him after they'd released the old lad, and his use of the English language was an eye-opener to say the least. I won't tell you where he suggested I shove the wooden frame, but I assure you it would have been an impossible feat.

We hadn't left Manchester yet and already the vacation was looking rather peculiar. The ten and a half hours we spent waiting for an aeroplane at Heathrow wasn't calculated to make us double up with unbridled merriment, either.

As if reluctantly, British Airways beckoned to our unhappy band that the flight to St Lucia was at last ready to be boarded, and it was at that moment I found that I'd lost the bits of card that enable you to get on the sky-liner.

My family were kept waiting as the other more intelligent passengers climbed the steel stairs to await transport to far pavilions, whilst I scoured seats and floors looking for the bloody boarding cards. By this time my wife was sick of our marriage and the kids didn't like me any more. A man shouted at me several times that the plane would have to go without us. Fortunately, before I found the strength to scream, my younger daughter's little shoulder bag fell to the floor and the first things that fell out were the boarding cards, closely followed by a doll's right arm and a grimy toffee. It took the combined strength of the family plus six airport officials to prevent me throttling my daughter, and there was talk of a sedative.

The other passengers glared at us, the air crew glared at us, and a stony-faced stewardess fastened my seat belt so tightly my tongue shot out.

The in-flight movie was a 'disaster' one in which an aeroplane sank under the Pacific, and my son decided that he had better inform his parents that he had developed acute diarrhoea.

We were to be met at the St Lucia airport and transported by luxury coach to our hotel. The first sound we heard as, feeling wobbly, we trooped off the aircraft, was the melancholy drone of an artillery piece closely followed by a loud whoosh and boom. Oh, I nearly forgot to mention, it was raining like hell. Armed men pushed us through the customs without a sign of a calypso, and the truth emerged: there was a riot taking place. The luxury coach was now ready for the knacker's yard after getting in the way of a mortar. Two First World War army lorries took a cargo of near-hysterical tourists to their hotels via a banana plantation, and the curtain of heavy tropical rain ensured that we saw bugger all.

Our hotel looked as if the jungle was devouring it, and as the rain abated, a chorus of bull frogs started up. A scream from inside our room indicated that Meg had gazed upon her first lizard, which was posing against a section of floral wallpaper, and Pamela hooted with delight as she caught a cockroach under a glass tumbler. My wife flatly refused to go to bed and sat up all night with a broom handle. As I was being shunned by the family, I decided to go out on to the beach. A watery sun had begun to peep from behind a bank of dark nimbus and my spirits lifted.

The children joined me, and as large waves began to nudge the shore, I lectured them on the inadvisability of using surf boards without the appropriate tuition. Just then, a wave of some fifteen feet or more toppled over me, throwing me up then down, tossing me like a minnow one minute, wrestling me to the seabed the next. Stunned and half drowned, I floated like the carcass of a whale until the family stopped laughing and had the good sense to pull me on to the sand. A fussy black doctor called me an idiot under his breath and tersely informed yours truly that I had cracked two ribs and would have to be strapped up.

The capital of St Lucia is a smelly dump (well, it was then) called Castries and most of it was boarded up, so it was Thanks Be To God that after three nights of steel bands, insect bites, baritone frogs and darting lizards, malaria, beri-beri and potential leprosy, my tight-lipped, pale family and I staggered up the gangplank and kissed the decks of the good ship SS *Countess*. The wife and children were sea-sick the moment the ship glided away from the harbour, and I spent two wonderful days and nights getting absolutely pissed with anybody who would drink with me. I had purchased a superb and expensive camera with which to record this momentous trip, and in Venezuela as I posed the family under the celebrated statue of Simon Bolívar, somebody's foot got in the way of my appendage and I fell in front of a shabby taxi. The driver braked, his rusty conveyance knocked over a fruit stall, and somebody called me 'a gringo bastardo'. Incidentally, the camera was in bits; no photographs to bore the relatives with.

My son's diarrhoea was the talk of the ship and several sensitive people suggested a long period of quarantine or a court martial. The smell from our cabin and his trousers became quite unbearable and on at least one occasion he was attacked with an air freshener. The swimming pool was never used despite the rather hot weather, and I couldn't understand why until one morning I jumped in – I have known cold in the past but nothing to compare with the freezing waters of that pool. Within seconds my skin was a deep blue colour and my genitals had shrunk, never to resume their former health.... to this very day I can only enjoy sex with the aid of a radar beam to locate the equipment of desire. Throughout this disaster I only had to look into Meg's eyes and laughter took over....

The liner docked at San Juan, Puerto Rico, and I hired a taxi to show the family the sights. It gave me an excellent opportunity to practise my Spanish, and the driver, a fierce little man with a facial boil, congratulated me heartily. At the end of the trip I gave him a tip, and to my astonishment he damned near kissed my sandals. When he drove off I realised why – in his currency I'd given him a hundred pound note. I ran after the taxi shouting 'Spanish bastardo!' The cab sprouted an arm on the end of which two fingers were raised. The rest of the ill-fated, doom-laden vacation was spent vomiting as the ship crashed through mountainous seas, and I inherited my son's diarrhoea.

That is why I am not very fond of travelling!

Going up and down the motorway every week was driving me nuts, and at the close of the season I wasn't sorry to see the back of *Blankety Blank* for a bit.

Julie came home from Nottingham on an extended leave because, although domestic nurses came every day to wash Meg and tend to any soreness she was getting from sitting too long, Julie wanted to be with her mother. It was a boon for the family that Julie also took over the cooking: my efforts at the culinary art were so bad. I once tossed a pancake – I've no idea what I put in the mixture, but for three months I used it as a pelmet.

By this time only will power was enabling Meg to walk even a few yards. Something had to be done.

Meanwhile, the pantomime season was upon us. That year, thanks to some adroit bargaining by my agents,

Norman Murray and Anne Chudleigh, I was headlining in Manchester at the magnificent Palace Theatre. The panto was *Babes in the Wood*, my favourite of all time. Also on the bill were Ruth Madoc of *Hi De Hi* fame (playing principal boy); John Nettles, a classically trained actor who was enjoying television success with a detective series called *Bergerac* (playing the villainous Sheriff of Nottingham); my lovable inventions, the Roly Polys, two stars of children's television, Mark Curry and John Noakes, from *Blue Peter*, and a fine young singer, Louise English, as Maid Marion. I, of course, was billed as Nurse Ada, which meant I had a free rein to do what I fancied ... within reason.

Rehearsals started in London and it gave me the chance to carry out my duties as King Rat and attend Lodge. To be King Rat in the Grand Order of Water Rats is an honour and a privilege. To be chosen by one's own profession, it is a true accolade and tribute from one's peers. After rehearsals in a gloomy church hall in Lambeth, a place so old the woodworm spoke Latin, I would dash off to various venues to help raise money for the charities that most concerned the Rats, and to oversee the monthly Lodge, which consisted of facts, figures, fun and comradeship.

Whilst I was rehearsing, I was absolutely thrilled to receive an invitation to attend a function at Buckingham Palace. Meg had been invited, too, and although I was informed that a ramp was available for wheelchairs, she declined the offer and I fully understood.

Rehearsals were not going that well.... For a start, John Nettles had broken his leg whilst filming and so he was hopping about the dusty, depressing rehearsal-room on a crutch that must have seen service in *Treasure Island*.

As an actor John was quite superb, but at first I had the

distinct impression that pantomime was not his forte and that the idea of a legitimate actor working as a double act with a variety comic did not seem to sit well with him. But how wrong I was. He was superb. All the stuff we did together was magic.

With rehearsals over, I would drag myself across from South London – not my favourite part of the Great Metropolis – to my Marble Arch hotel, where I would telephone home to see how Meg was. It was a ritual.

I left the rehearsal-room early the day I was due to attend Buck House, and it was just as well I did for the traffic had snarled into a static, choking, metal snake. The Lord only knows how long it had been stuck on Chelsea Bridge, but there was a car in front of me with a nodding dog in the rear window – and it was a skeleton.

I've never seen anything like it – they were even clamping pedestrians. Inside the cab I inwardly fumed. Tonight I was due to enter Buckingham Place – a dream – but if I didn't get out of this foul-up soon, I'd be so late for the 'do' Prince Charles would be on the throne. God bless the cabbie I had ... he weaved and twirled around odd little backwaters and eventually got me to my hotel with only forty-five minutes to spare. I went across to the taxi rank to book a cab for later, and when I informed the cabbie of our destination, he sprang to attention and gasped, 'Gawd blimey, Les, this is a job for the Merc.'

Half an hour later, after a shower, a change into something more appropriate for the occasion, and two or three large whiskies, I sallied forth from the hotel, and there, gleaming seductively, was an old Mercedes saloon. My cabbie stood by the rear passenger door, wearing a black peaked cap and leather boots. He looked like something out of a pre-war German movie. He saluted and said: 'I fort 'ard do it in style, guv.' I grinned. 'You look great, my old china, and now, let us away to the Palace.' He smiled as other cab drivers made rude remarks at him. 'F . . . awf,' he said winningly, and we rumbled away towards our destination.

It was only after being escorted up the red carpeted stairs to the reception saloon, that I happened to look down and noticed that in my haste to make myself presentable I'd put on two different shoes – both black, but different in design. Here I was in Buckingham Palace, in the company of nobility and captains of industry, and my shoes stuck out like a sore thumb. It was a splendid evening: every time I held out an empty glass, a smart flunkey in a colourful frogged jacket would whip it away and hand me a replenished tumbler. At one point in the festivity, Prince Philip called me over and said with an air of amusement: 'Did you know you've got two odd shoes on?' I couldn't resist it. I replied, 'Yes, sir, and I've got a pair just like these at home.' The Prince roared; I thanked God for enabling me to remember the old joke.

I knew I was getting pissed but on I carried, talking a lot of crap and leering at all the ladies. Mercifully for my liver, bulky men started to usher us out and I dimly recall telling one of them that I had a black belt at judo. My driver poured me into the Mercedes and left me sitting on the steps of the hotel singing 'We all live in a yellow submarine'.

My year as King Rat was drawing to a close, and the annual November Rats' Ball at the Grosvenor House Hotel was looming on the horizon. Meg wanted to go to it along with the rest of the family, and I was very pleased that she had agreed to go. Her health seemed to be holding well, although she had started to complain about her vision. She said she was experiencing trouble in focusing.

The Rats' Ball is a big social occasion. Any star of stage, television or film worth his or her salt, must be there on that gala night, and on that November evening in 1986, there was a positive galaxy of celebrities milling around the Great Room. It is the custom that all the past King Rats and their ladies, as well as the current King Rat, of course, parade across the vast dance floor at the beginning of the evening, take a bow, then go to their respective tables.

As I wheeled Meg across the floor, the entire audience rose to its feet and the applause was deafening. I could feel the love in that room all directed to my wife, a brave and well respected lady. Stars like Michael Caine, Michael Crawford, Warren Mitchell, and Robert Powell to name but a few, surrounded her, and she held court with radiant dignity.

With all due modesty, I have to say that my after-dinner speech went extremely well. I was followed by Dr Christiaan Barnard, the pioneer of heart transplant surgery. Although a controversial man, I found him to be warm and likeable; the only thing that disturbed me was the intensity with which he looked at Meg, for I well knew that Christiaan Barnard was a brilliant doctor. At the end of his speech the good doctor thanked me, then turned to Meg, held her hand, and said in a voice of such compassion: 'You are truly, Mrs Dawson, one of the bravest people I have ever met.' I saw something in his eyes and my blood chilled, and the rest of the night sped by without my really being a part of it.

They tell me that the Ball was an unqualified success, regarded by many fellow Rats as one of the very best of the last ten years or so.... Certainly there did seem to be a party atmosphere and high spirits. I presented David

Jason with an award, I danced with famous ladies and joked with famous men ... but I didn't feel a part of it. I remembered the look in Christiaan Barnard's eyes.

Rehearsals ended in London and it was time to finish off in Manchester. I was moved to find Meg waiting at the door for me in her chair when I tumbled out of the taxi. She put her arms around me and whispered: 'I love you.'

I travelled every day from St Annes to Manchester with Mo and Marie, two of the Roly Polys, and it was a great relief to know that I could keep my eye on Meg's condition, which was worsening. I had bought a little vehicle called a Nissan Prairie and I'd had an electric lift installed in the passenger seat so that Meg could sit in her wheelchair on the ramp of the lift, and be raised into the car without moving from her chair ... because by now, Meg could no longer walk at all. Her legs had lost all feeling. At least I could take her out either for a spin in the countryside or along the promenade, or for her favourite pursuit – shopping. The van gave her a renewed interest and it was money well spent.

Before opening in the pantomime, which was already a record sell-out, it was time to peddle my latest literary offering: *A Time Before Genesis*. It was my first attempt at writing a serious novel, and naturally I was more than a bit apprehensive as to how it would be received, for after all we do tend to put people in boxes, do we not, and therefore could a comedian writing a serious work be taken seriously?

I won't go into detail about the novel, suffice to say that it is about things that have always intrigued me: religion, after-life, alien influences – they were just some of the themes I attempted to explore in my book. I had done two years' research and studied the Bible and a translation of the Koran before writing a word. Philosophy kept me burning the midnight oil, and paranormal theories I devoured like food.

My publishers at the time, Elm Tree Books, had agreed to publish the novel only on condition that I also wrote my autobiography. It was a hell of an undertaking, but I desperately wanted to see my novel in print so I readily agreed to start on my autobiography as well. Couple all this with pantomime, radio work and TV and it will give you some idea of how crippling a workload I had set myself. Little wonder, then, that later on, my body would rebel.

If that wasn't enough, my agents happily informed me that I had been offered a cabaret date in New York! There were just nine days to go before we opened the pantomime in Manchester, but how could I turn down the chance to go to the States?

It was a good deal: an excellent fee for the gig, and the return trip from Heathrow to Kennedy by Concorde! Meg said, 'Go, love, you may never be asked again if you turn it down.' What a lady.

My agents got me out of the rehearsals for *Babes in the Wood* by some jiggery pokery, I suspect, and off I jetted in the finest aeroplane the world has ever seen.

I cannot describe the feeling of pride I felt as I sat in that mighty aircraft. The statistics were incredible: the flight time from London to New York just three hours twenty-five minutes! Speed, 1,760 miles per hour.... Height, 68,000 feet. The food served on board was magnificent and Dom Perignon champagne was served in an endless circuit by gorgeous stewardesses. I drank more than my share of that most delectable of nectars.

All at once the flight was coming to an end. Below

me I could see the million shining lights of the soaring metropolis. Towering fingers of concrete with glittering arcs of light around them; ribbons lighting the passage of traffic could be seen quite clearly ... and suddenly there was a concerto of outraged rubber and screeching tarmac as we touched down.

Kennedy Airport New York, Babylon revisited: unfamiliar accents both loud and strident demanding to know what goods or treasures one is bringing through the customs; travellers from every nation jostling for attention; hot children with taut expressions; travellers with empty eyes watching other travellers.... From Kennedy we fly by helicopter to Manhattan Island, purchased from the Indians for glass beads.

It is by the side of a main road, slightly underneath a bridge, that the romance ends. It is dirty and cold and there isn't a taxi in sight to take us into the heart of Downtown Manhattan.... Too many violent movies cause us to eye with apprehension the slightest suggestion of movement in the shadows. A yellow, grime-streaked cab finally brakes to a halt in a nimbus of choking exhaust gases, and a swarthy face with a drooping moustache peers at you, and when the face speaks, you are reminded, as George Bernard Shaw once said, that Great Britain and America are two countries separated by the same language....

It takes an age to reach our destination. I'm not for one second impugning the honesty of that New York taxi driver, but I get the distinct impression he has driven us to the city centre via Detroit.

Eventually we alight at our destination: the Westbury Hotel on Madison Avenue, where I will be appearing as well as staying. It's a high class inn and friendly, so what better place to test out this new found warmth than the beckoning womb of the bar. My agents, Norman and Anne, who had cleverly included themselves on this sojourn, totter to bed, whilst I sample the delights of several large Jack Daniel's.... To my surprise upon entering my suite I found two messages awaiting attention on the bedside table. One was from Peter Stringfellow, the nightclub owner from London, and one from my childhood friend, Ken Cowx, who was now a translator at the United Nations. I phoned them both up and made arrangements to see the pair of them the next evening. Having telephoned home as per the norm and having been reassured that all is well, I spend an hour watching television and sit stunned at the sheer awesome idiocy of it. I could feel a chill of apprehension that this screened garbage will one day, alas, find its way on to British screens as the grip of the accountant tightens on artistic budgets.... It is a depressing thought to go to bed on, but still, there is tomorrow to explore the city.

One thing that still bothered me was, what was a Northern red-nosed comedian doing, appearing in the United States? Next morning a car arrived at the hotel door and I was whisked away to find out.... In a penthouse office suite so posh the mice wore powdered wigs, high above Fifth Avenue, I met the man who had engaged me. He turned out to be a multi-millionaire oil and insurance tycoon, and he wanted me to perform to an invited audience of wealthy socialites and business people. It sounded daunting, and I still wondered: why me? As if sensing my unspoken question, my host flashed a wide smile, poured me another Jack Daniel's and said:

'You are probably wondering, Les, why I booked you for the cabaret?'

I nodded.

'I asked my wife what she most wanted for a Christmas present, and she answered, "I'd like to see and hear Les Dawson, darling".' He smiled at my expression. 'It's true, Les – you are a Christmas gift for my wife.'

Thunderstruck is a reasonably accurate description of my reaction to this – I've been some things in my time, but never a Christmas box!

It turned out that his wife was a Yorkshirewoman from Leeds and she was homesick for the things she'd left behind: Yorkshire pudding, Northern beer, her friends and family, and ... Les Dawson.

We left the tycoon's swish penthouse and I hired a stretch limo to tour the city.

The driver, who hailed from the Bronx, was a voluble guide, and I saw the Battery, Greenwich Village, Chinatown, the Bowery, Central Park; he was glowing with enthusiasm for his New York ... until I asked him to take me through Harlem. His reponse was on the lines of 'Jeeze, feller, you gotta be a Limey ... *Harlem* for Christ's sake?' I mildly pointed out that it was only three-thirty in the afternoon and surely we'd be safe. 'Harlem is never safe, pal,' he moaned, but I persuaded him finally just to creep into the perimeter of the infamous ghetto ...

It was well worth the extra fifteen dollars that I bribed him with, for going through Harlem was an education. I've known poverty – I experienced it as a child in Manchester – but ours was a physical poverty. What I saw in Harlem was a spiritual poverty that was etched on the faces of young and old alike, from the despairing countenance of an elderly black lady slumped on a tenement door step, to the hate-filled expressions of a street gang lounging atop a heap of broken bricks and cement. Civilisation, December 1985.

As we drove by, they eyed the car with sullen mistrust and one of them threw a bottle at the vehicle and a stream of abuse followed in its wake. My driver's nerves were shot to hell and I could see that he desperately wanted to end this trip and be rid of one insane Limey. In Spanish Harlem a battered 1950s Buick suddenly pulled alongside our limo and my driver very nearly commenced to evacuate his bowels.

'Hey man.' This from the swarthy hoodlum in the passenger seat. 'You wanna race, mi amigo? . . . Wassamatter, you a big man – too big for the likes of a Spick?'

My driver was whimpering as he slowly drove along, with the Buick cruising at his side. By this time interested people were oozing out of rancid boltholes and glaring at the cavalcade; but the most intense hostility was concentrated on our clean stretch limo.

It was time to do something to ease this rapidly deteriorating situation. . . . Almost without thinking, I poked my head through the window and shouted: 'Hello, chaps' in an over-the-top English accent. 'I say, nice of you to chat, we seem a trifle off course, could you kindly direct us to Central Park?'

The mouths of the yobs dropped open and one of them, I swear, damn nearly saluted. The upshot was they didn't simply direct us to Central Park, they indicated that we should follow them, which we did, and lo and behold! there we were at the Park. My driver couln't stop muttering: 'Damn. . . . Sons of bitches. . . .' As he dropped me off at the hotel, he wrung my hand like a wet leather, warbling, 'Jeeze, man, am I glad to know ya, pal. . . . God damn Limey! . . . Thanks buddy. . . .' Well, words to that effect.

I've never been so proud of being British, but I wouldn't have been quite so cocksure if I'd known that the day before in Spanish Harlem two men had gunned down a suspected police informer.

The thought of my debut on the morrow kept me awake all night. Just what the hell was I going to do for the confounded Yanks? It wasn't until dawn appeared that I knew what course to take.

I decided to perform my act rather like a lecture instead of trying to get by with ordinary patter, which I felt would be obscure to the Americans – judging by what passed for humour on their television shows, I might as well read out a passage from Chekov for all the laughs I'd get. The die was cast. . . . I rehearsed with a gum-chewing trio with nasal problems and suddenly it was showtime!

The elegant room was full of beefy, well-tailored men and classically gowned ladies. One could almost smell money in the wreaths of cigar smoke that hung in garlands above the tables ... a short introduction from a compère who looked a bit like the late Alan Ladd, and the porky comedian from the North of England began. . . .

'Good evening, ladies and gentlemen, it is an honour to be here in New York, which I've found is a sort of Pittsburg with a sneer.'

'The first thing to remember is that I am from the crucible of civilisation and you are merely colonials.'

'I can't understand why you wanted independence, I've seen Boston ... in my opinion the Indians should have dumped Boston and kept the tea.'

The opening lines kept them quiet, if a trifle puzzled, and I went on:

'My hotel is full of lady golfers: three times now a dame has approached me saying that she's a hooker.'

'My wife is outside in the car – I would have brought her in but I've lost the keys to the trunk.'

'My hotel is very old-fashioned, it's decorated in early Confederate.'

I got by, though I didn't exactly slay them. However, my off-key piano playing won the day as it were, and the tycoon's wife said, 'Eeh, that were grand, our Les', and a heavily lined lady who reeked of gin slapped me on the back and yelled, 'Listen, kid, why doncha become a comic?'

The return to the UK was as smooth as the flight going out, and I caught the shuttle to Manchester still as fresh as a daisy with none of the usual jet lag problems associated with ordinary aeroplane travels.

As soon as the children saw me they voiced their worries about Meg. If they had known the truth that I was living with.... Stuart, Julie and Pamela were putting on a brave face and my heart went out to them, but I knew that in their bedrooms they prayed and cried. Despair was showing in their faces, and the daily sight of their mother's agony was maturing them rapidly.

Meg greeted me fondly, but the lines of pain were showing in her face. It was now quite impossible for her to get up the stairs, so a small bed was brought down and put into the study for her. Even the trips in the Nissan gave her extreme discomfort now, and sometimes I had to harden my heart and virtually force her into the wheelchair, if only to give her a change of scenery from four walls.

To keep her spirits alive, I would deliberately say something that would irritate her and she'd play merry hell with me, but at least it kept her fighting.... Mind you, after I'd done this sort of thing with her, I would go upstairs and sob my heart out; but I firmly believe that when someone is ill, they should be angry about it. I've seen people stricken by cancer who meekly give in and adopt a pious, fatalistic kind of attitude: 'What will be will be', 'God works in mysterious ways'.... Baloney! Be angry, say '*Why me?*' It is my contention that directed and purposeful anger is good for the body cells and the brain. As the old axiom says, 'God helps those who help themselves'. At any rate, anger worked for my wife when her spirits sank under the weight of pain. I made it clear that relatives, friends and neighbours should be cheerful and nonchalant, not heavy and doom-laden.

Meanwhile, the pantomime was getting under way with final rehearsals, and soon the day of the Dress Rehearsal dawned.... We were to have an invited audience of deprived children for this, and although it was looked upon as the dress run, to me, even though it was a free show for the kids, it was a performance, and it had to be just right.

Tears in the Laughter

The audience saw the little fat man in the outrageous nurse's outfit prance on to the stage. He had a huge joke syringe pinned to his costume, he wore a ridiculous wig, and the end of his nose was painted bright red.

They saw him perform a silly pretend trip as he entered the glare of the lights, and they watched as he craned forwards over the footlights and said:

'Hello, kids! I'm Nurse Ada and I have three children.... One of each.'

'I love children, I used to go to school with them.'

'If you see two flies on the wallpaper, which one is the bandit? It's the one making for the border.'

'I have a dog with no nose.... How does it smell? Awful.'

The audience saw the little fat man make the kids laugh. What they didn't see was the little fat man in his dressing-room, alone with his tortured thoughts as he repeatedly telephoned home to ask how much pain his wife was in.

Old Nettles and I got on now like a house on fire and he was picking up the tricks of pantomime very quickly, as he realised just how difficult a pantomime is to stage successfully. After all, what other form of production has to weld together dancers, singers, actors, comedians and children in one show?

We opened just before Christmas.... As on every first night, nerves were jangling and tension was all around – quite a bit of it in my dressing-room, because here I was, headlining in my home town.... How would I be received? Would I lay an enormous egg? I reached for the bottle of Scotch.

The overture begins; the audience clears its throat; late-comers sheepishly make for their seats.... Backstage the children take their positions for the village scene.... The principals wait and listen in anticipation of the initial reaction.

All seems to go well. The music is bright and the songs tuneful. The little kids are enchanting and already some female members of the audience are giving vent to 'Oooohs' and 'Aaahhs'. They love the children. The little beasts are stealing the show already!

John Nettles enters on a horse. It is a magnificent entrance and gets a huge ovation.... Play-on music for me, Nurse Ada. Nurse's outfit with comic appliances crossed over massive bosom. Wig swept back into a large bun, red nose on which are perched bifocals.... Original script forgotten, it's ad lib time, folks....

> *'What a thrill to be in Manchester.... Birmingham with O levels.'*
>
> *'You'll find that this show is, oh, what's the word I'm looking for? Oh yes, crap.'*
>
> *'A duck went into a chemist's shop, he said, "A tube of Lipsyl, please." The chemist said, "Certainly, that will be 50p." The duck said, "Well, put it on my bill." '*
>
> *'Where would we all be without a laugh? Here.'*
>
> *'I do get the odd smile from an audience, but it's usually wind.'*

'Where are you from, Missus? Cardiff? You won't be used to all this – carpets and electricity– will you?'

'Put a bloody smile on your face, sir, you look like a bulldog chewing a wasp.'

That's a short version of my opening that night. I pulled the theatre to pieces, the management, the guys backstage ('They're all shiftworkers – if you mention work, they shift'). The dancers, I said, were from a foot clinic, and that John Nettles was about as much good as an actor as Kojak was selling home perms. The first night audience roared, even though what I was saying bore no relation to the panto.

Then came the scene between Nettles and Dawson, which in the original text had been a very dreary piece indeed. Now we did our version....

ME: Why, it's John Nettles, loosely disguised as the Sheriff of Nottingham. Last time I saw a face like that, there was a hook in it.
JOHN: She can talk, last time I saw a face and figure like hers, the owner was being milked.... If she lived in India, she'd be sacred.
ME: You remind me of the sea.
JOHN: You mean I'm wild, restless and untamed?
ME: No.... You make me sick.
JOHN: You remind me of a Viking.
ME: Really? Do you mean blonde and beautiful?
JOHN: No.... You've got a face like a Norse.
ME: Tell you what, I could live in your eyes.
JOHN: Well, you'd be at home ... there's a sty in one of them.

The show overran by half an hour and the audience bayed for more. I had drunk rather more than I should have done and my curtain speech was a trifle botched, one might say. However, we were all cock-a-hoop with the way the panto had gone and I waited for Paul Elliot, the Producer, to come into the dressing-room and pat me on the head. He never came in, and I was worried that the extent of my ad-libbing had upset him.

Later, at the first night party, Paul went round slapping people on the back but I was seemingly ignored. 'Stuff him,' I decided, and commenced to drink the bar dry. Only at the end of the evening did Paul finally confront me.... 'I've left you until last because I couldn't find a word greater than magnificent ... absolutely magnificent,' he said, and walked off.

The reviews for the show came out on Christmas Eve. All of them, both local and national reviews, raved over the show saying that it was the funniest panto in years and a 'must' for the family. One critic wrote: 'Thoroughly enjoyable pantomime, Les Dawson is the best Dame I have ever seen, he's certainly the finest one this century!' He went on: 'The script was what we had come to expect so it's a good job that Dawson ad-libbed most of it.'

John Nettles received wonderful notices, as did Ruth Madoc, and I was overjoyed. Later that day the telephone rang. It was Paul Elliot. He wished us all a Merry Christmas and said, 'Thanks for showing me that my original misgivings about your ad-libbing were wrong.... Congratulations.' It takes a big man to say that and I'm proud to count him as a friend.

I was able to be with Meg every night but her health was no better despite the increased medication. Now she was totally bedridden and thank God I was working otherwise my heart would have broken. I was drinking too much again and punishing myself.... Thoughts tormented me constantly. Had I done enough for her? Was I doing enough for her? Over and over again I would curse God and deny Him.... Then I would pray to Him.

The children still didn't know that one day we would lose her and I hadn't the heart to tell them. Then I came home one night and found her sitting up and laughing with the kids and she looked a picture of health! 'Thank you, God,' I whispered. She seemed to rally with every passing day and the pain appeared to have gone altogether.

The production of *Babes in the Wood* came to a successful close, having broken all previous records and gone very smoothly indeed – well, apart from one odd incident.

I had read earlier on in the run that Princess Michael of Kent was coming to see the pantomime with some children. Obviously I was thrilled and delighted by the news, but I thought it strange that the theatre management hadn't informed me first instead of my having to read about it in the *Manchester Evening News*. I rang the theatre administration office and they shrugged the whole thing off as a bit of a nuisance. Of course, the penny dropped. The Manchester City Council were extremely left wing in their politics, to the extent that the Lord Mayor was now known as the 'First Chair Person'. What an ugly, grey phrase!

The Princess arrived at the theatre for the matinée and there wasn't a flower for her or a proper delegation to meet her. She roared with laughter at the show and at the interval the administrator came backstage to ask me what the procedure would be after the matinée, as the Princess wished to meet the cast. By the way he said it I knew he didn't give a damn, so I replied coldly, 'I will arrange for the whole cast to remain on stage after the performance, I shall then wait at the pass door for the Princess and I shall introduce her to the cast.' I couldn't believe my ears when the administrator said testily, 'Oh, you don't need the whole lot there, Les. Just you and Nettles and Ruth Madoc.' With disgust in my voice I pointed out that that would be a breach of courtesy, and that all the children would be overjoyed to meet a real live Princess.

The curtain closed, the cast lined up, and I told them that the protocol was they said their name when introduced to the Princess, thus avoiding any embarrasing moment.

I greeted Princess Michael, whom I'd had the great pleasure of meeting on several previous occasions, and the whole affair went well. The Princess gripped my arm tightly as we left the stage: there in the wings, in a tight knot, were the tabloid press who had recently accused her of having a father who had been a member of the German SS. How a baby girl of two could be held responsible for her father's actions is quite beyond me. . . .

One of the more sordid hacks asked me if it was true that I had once kissed the Princess. I said it was; it had happened during the ovation I received from my fellow Water Rats upon being made King Rat. The Princess and her husband Prince Michael were guests of honour that night, and the Princess had clapped delightedly and sort of leaned forward with the side of her face to the fore. Without thinking I had bent over and held her hands, and kissed her lightly on the cheek. This faux pas had brought cheers; I couldn't apologise enough, but Prince Michael had taken it all with high good humour.

That is what I told that 'journalist', and two days later I received a telephone call in the dressing-room from Princess Michael's press official, saying that the Princess was very hurt by what she had read in this tabloid, namely, that she had kissed me full on the lips. From all accounts – and quite rightly so – she was very irate about it and was considering a lawsuit against the newspaper in question. Luckily I managed to make the official realise that she would be better off ignoring it all. As I put it to him, 'Today's news is tomorrow's garbage.'

It had been a long and exhausting run and it was a relief to be at home for a while. There was no chance of a holiday but I'm a home bird and it didn't bother me. I felt satisfied with life; a successful pantomime behind me, television bookings ahead and a bank balance doing very nicely, thank you. Meg seemed much improved, and then fate decided that that was enough happiness. . . .

Meg and I were watching snooker on the television – it was by far her favourite programme – when she suddenly asked me to adjust the set.

'What's the matter with it?' I asked casually.

'It's blurred,' she said.

It wasn't blurred, the picture was perfect.

She got annoyed with me trying to test her sight, then she got angry with herself, as she was vainly rubbing her eyes to clear away the fuzz. Over the next two weeks, her eyesight worsened. I changed her spectacles but they made not a jot of difference. It was now the end of February and her health was on the decline again as before.

I took her down to Christie's for her check-up, and I mentioned that her eyes were bad and the specialist looked long and hard at me. They wheeled Meg away for the check-up and I read a magazine, then another one. . . . This was the longest time they'd been with her. I went outside and lit a cigarette. The receptionist said something like, 'Not to worry, they'll be giving her an eye test.' Of course, that was it, wasn't it? I sat, then I stood. . . . Hang on, they're coming back. . . . I can hear Meg laughing with the specialist. . . . Thank you, God, she's going to be all right, isn't she? Meg looked radiantly at me, and the specialist indicated that they wanted to speak to me whilst Meg had a well-earned cup of tea.

I followed them into another room. They were going to tell me what treatment would be prescribed for her eyes.... Yes, that's what they wanted to say, wasn't it?

The specialist and his colleague sat down and so did I.... Hey, why weren't they smiling and laughing now?

'I'm afraid we have bad news for you.... The cancer has spread behind the eyes. Your wife has only a few weeks....'

A few weeks for what? Is she going blind?

'The cancer has spread all over, Mr Dawson. It's only a matter of time.'

Holy Christ, what are you telling me? My wife is going to die and there's nothing you can do?

I felt as if someone had hit me from behind with a hammer. I couldn't catch my breath, and my heart faltered in an uneven tempo....

I saw genuine compassion on their faces.

'What do I do?' I asked them through dry lips.

'You must carry on as normal,' one of them said.

Carry on as normal? Just how the hell do I do that?

I couldn't stop the tears. There and then in front of those learned men, I cried bitter, frustrated tears.

Eventually I pulled myself together and rejoined Meg, who was chatting happily with the receptionist.

Somehow I got her into the Nissan and to all her questions I lied and lied. My head ached and my whole body was numb with fear and grief.

It was time to break the news to the children that their mother was going to die.

I told Pamela and she listened in silence, then ran up

to her room. I told our son Stuart, and he left the house to be alone with his grief.

I telephoned Julie at the hospital in Nottingham. She broke down on the phone and immediately made arrangements to come home.

The family were weaving a protective net around the little woman we all loved so very much.

I still couldn't take it in, and I decided to get a second opinion. I heard from a friend who had survived cancer that a doctor in Harley Street could work miracles and so I bundled Meg off to London....

It was, of course, a waste of time and effort. He took one look at her and silently shook his head.... No dialogue was needed.

I told my agents the bad news and they immediately cancelled all my bookings. Julie came home and helped the visiting nurses to bathe her mother and tend to her needs.

The immediate family was informed but they wisely didn't all flock to the house otherwise Meg would have suspected the worst. I couldn't tell too many people about her condition, in case the press got to know, and the last thing I wanted was them around.

Slowly, before our eyes, Meg began to fade from us. She looked so tiny and childlike as she lay in the bed, now unseeing, waiting to go. Occasionally she would rally but then she would sink again.

Outside, I remember, the wind howled and dashed whips of rain against the window of the room where she lay. We took it in turns now to sleep in the study near her, so as to be on hand for any deterioration.... And then the human spirit rises above its tortured clay, and now she smiles, seems more alert, and her facial colour returns.

In fact, in mid March, the biggest problem she was

tormented with was bed sores, which needed hourly attention.

I stopped looking in the bathroom mirror to shave: my eyes were sunken holes and black rimmed with tiredness, and my face had lost its roundness with the strain. It was Meg who urged me to go out with a friend for a drink, and with the kids quite able to tend to any sudden problem I started going out to my club on a Friday, and then on to the St Ives Hotel to finish off with a late drink.

I was drinking too much and feeling very sorry for myself. My appearance was causing comment; I dressed like a tramp and I acted in a very silly, hostile manner. The beautiful young woman behind the bar would listen to me whine and put up with my irresponsible attempts at humour with kindness and patience. I was becoming a self-suffering disgrace. I knew that friends were beginning to avoid my company; I was boring and sarcastic outside the house, indoors I was self-pitying and tearful, so much so that my wife rebuked me in front of the children.... I was totally abject.

March gave way to a mild April that shyly lightened the landscape with the promise of spring, but there was no happy anticipation in Garth House because we were losing Meg. Her family came frequently now to visit her, but most of the time she was not aware of their presence. Her world was a drugged, secret place where time was without pain and feeling.

Sitting by her bed, I would listen to her speak about her childhood; images and scenes recognised and remembered by her sisters. Once, in front of the family, she opened her eyes and stunned us all by describing the construction of a new public house and shopping mall, which she said she'd 'flown' over. Now, here is the most amazing part of this incident: Meg, who had never seen the work being carried out in St Annes Square, described in astonishing detail the new layout of the mall, the shape of the new public house ... it was uncanny.

Is it possible that we can detach our spirit energy from our physical body and voyage forth in a limitless, unrestricted dimension? Are we still on the threshold of understanding the electro-magnetic waves that we create?

Another strange incident occurred on the night of 12 April. Meg had been talking about the past, sometimes angrily, sometimes gently. Now and again she would snap her eyes open and look around at her family. 'Stuart, my son.... There's our Julie.... Pamela, is that you? Where's your dad? There's Les.' She would then become fierce with me as I knelt by the side of the bed holding her hand. 'Let me go.... I have to go,' she would say in great agitation. 'Come back to us, Meg,' I would reply. That night, as this interchange took place, some lumps of coloured glass imitation coals from the electric fire in the study suddenly leapt in the air and cascaded on to the carpet.... Not one of the family was near the fire at the time. I felt that something was telling me to stop begging Meg to hold on and come back to us. I felt a power drawing her to another realm that was beyond our understanding.

However, I still persisted in urging her to stay with us and she, poor dear lass, continued to beg me to let her go.

In the early hours of Tuesday 15 April 1986, at three minutes to seven, my younger daughter, who had been sleeping in the study with her mum – she had slept in that room more often than the rest of us – called to us that there was something wrong with Meg. We gathered around the bed on which my little wife lay, and saw that she was passing away from us. Her breathing became laboured but she was unconscious and at peace as she drifted into another place.... Meg Dawson was dead.

The kids were marvellous, it was I who ran from the study blinded by tears. I stood in the kitchen whimpering: 'Give me a sign, Meg.' Now this you can believe or not: I'm telling it because it happened. The one kitchen item she had never really come to grips with was the microwave oven. Meg mistrusted it completely. Now as I spoke those words: 'Give me a sign, Meg', the microwave oven suddenly 'pinged' – I was at least five feet away from it, and I was alone in that kitchen!

It could have been a fault on the appliance or perhaps someone had used it earlier on and hadn't switched it off properly, or maybe you'll say it was my imagination. All I know is that from that incident I found a strength of will that I hadn't possessed before. I went back into the study and told the children to draw the curtains back and put their record players on.... I wanted sunlight in the room where she had died because she had been a sunny person.... I needed to hear music, preferably loud and with a beat that would bring life back into a house of death.

I was amazed by the number of people who called at the house in genuine sorrow.... I had never realised how many lives my Meg had touched.

I was overwhelmed by the masses of floral tributes, from friends and relatives and strangers. Telegrams arrived from all over the world, including one from Buckingham Palace which read simply:

Buckingham Palace

PLEASE ACCEPT MY DEEPEST CONDOLENCES ON YOUR VERY SAD LOSS

PHILIP

There was a chill in the air and a light, misty rain on the day of Meg's funeral. The service was at the Lytham Crematorium but at the children's request Meg was to be buried, so that any one of the family could go along and chat with her at times of anguish.... I thought it was a nice idea. Over two hundred and fifty people attended the service, not counting the hordes of good folk standing outside in the rain. There were show business stars, neighbours, close friends, acquaintances, immediate family and distant relatives.... Strangers came and wrung my hand. From them, I heard stories of deeds undertaken by my wife....

The little old lady who told me how Meg would call and give her provisions....

The elderly gentleman who ran a small charitable organisation for disabled folk, taking them for a free lunch. Meg was his main driver....

The good ladies from Meals on Wheels ... a similar group told me how much Meg had done for them, taking the very aged for little trips in her car....

As the stories unfolded, I realised that my wife's life had been one of giving to others.... I hadn't really completely known the woman I had married all those years ago.

Floral tributes ... so many for one small lady. I was only dimly aware of the newspaper reporters running across damp burial mounds, their ill-kempt photographers eagerly snapping every tear and show of grief.

I held Pamela close as we walked to Meg's last resting place. My mind was a turmoil of questions and despair. . . . As the coffin began its descent into the earth I placed a white rose on the lid and whispered, 'I will always love you – and please look after us all, darling.'

Does that sound a stupid thing to say? It probably does, of course, but I had that feeling that Meg was still around . . . and something was to happen that only confirmed this view.

As the casket descended, I remembered. . . .

1958, I meet Meg at a club where I am appearing. She's engaged to another guy. . . . We don't like each other on sight. She says, 'Do you want to use the clavoline?' (This was something that was fastened to the piano and could reproduce the sound of an organ.) And old smart arse here says, 'No love, I've just been.'

1960, 25 June. . . . We are wed at St Thomas's church in Crumpsall, and after the reception held in a pub, we set off for Austria on our honeymoon. The soaring peaks and fine wines and the long nights of love and getting to know one another. . . . All the good years to come. The shared poverty in our early marriage, the shared disappointments, the tragic miscarriages . . . many bad times but all good years together. The triumphs and the flops . . . we shared them all, and now I've lost her, my Meg, aged 48 years – that's all she had, 48 summers and winters, and now she's gone . . . and with her my life as well.

The funeral feast, for want of a better phrase for that most odious of customs, was held in the St Ives Hotel. The sight of the food made me sick; instead, I drank – a lot. Suddenly before me stood the beautiful young woman who worked behind the bar and who had been so kind to me when I'd been in my alcoholic states.

'I'm very sorry about your loss, Les,' she said softly, and her enormous eyes were full of moist compassion. She didn't have to say anything more but I knew by her look that she understood.

I walked away hurriedly to the toilet. I had to be alone.

Of course the popular press had a field day. In every major newspaper and the tabloids there was some comment, ranging from 'Agony of a Comic', to 'Les loses his Meg'. One that really hurt me with its cold prose was: 'Comic's wife killed by cancer'.

Another thing that convinced me that Meg's spirit energy was still around was the presence of the sweet smell of freesias ... her favourite flower. The scent of it could be detected all over the house, particularly in the kitchen, and once again I speculated on the possibility that when we slough off the physical body, we go into some sort of limbo in order to adjust to our new change of energy matter, and possibly assist the living to come to terms with their loss.

One thing I do know for certain is that it helped me to pull myself together and face the reality that I had lost my wife for ever.... I would never see her again.

The children were marvellous, and for their sake I had to put on a braver face than I felt like wearing.

Time does dull; it doesn't heal, but before long I had accepted that Meg wasn't around any more. No more would I hear her wheeling down the hall giving out instructions.... I decided to become mum and dad for the kids. I would fill both posts.

One incident made me realise what terrible anguish can boil beneath an apparently calm exterior.... Pamela, my younger daughter, took a lot of sleeping pills. Luckily, as it turned out, she hadn't taken enough to do any harm.

When I asked her why she'd done it, she said sadly, 'I didn't intend to kill myself, Dad. I thought if I took more than I should, perhaps I'd just be able to see mum one more time.'

Time dulls . . . it doesn't heal.

I found that people react most strangely to someone who has lost someone dear to them. Let me explain.

I did the shopping in the mornings, hoping to get finished before well-meaning neighbours and the other shoppers were about. Don't get me wrong, their concern was wonderful, but you can't stop in the middle of taking a tin of baked beans off a shelf in order to grunt and relive the loss for somebody else's benefit. The oddest thing I found was that people would approach me, bend slightly from the waist then peer up my nose and say earnestly: 'How are you coping with things?' 'It must be hard for you, love.' 'How are the children taking it?' 'Do you miss Meg, love?' 'God works in mysterious ways, doesn't he?'

There was a lighter side. From elderly ladies I learned the art of finding a tin of produce that hadn't been stamped with an increased price! One old woman dragged me to a heaped column of tinned peas, and with incredible dexterity, removed a dozen layers until, grunting with triumph, she produced a battered tin that was one penny cheaper than the others. . . . She had beaten the system.

I learned how to tell a good tomato from a bad one; my aged mentors taught me how to prod, fondle, poke and sniff out the better product. After such tuition, you couldn't pass *me* off with a duff melon! No haddock shoved under my nose could lie about its age, and I could gauge the weight of a chicken with one furtive pinch. I became an expert at choosing the best cut of beef; I wallowed in my new-found expertise at picking out the better fruits.... In a state of high exaltation I would troop along with my batch of old ladies to different supermarkets in order to save twopence on a jar of roughcut marmalade. I would stand in a darkened corner of Safeways and hug myself with glee at finding a jar of gravy granules threepence cheaper than the ones at Tesco's. I spent hours with my basket gossiping with my tottering old girls and I learned many dark secrets of the parish.

I had a lady doing for me, but frankly she wasn't a great success. She would prowl around the Hoover as if the thing might suddenly rear up and bite her. She used a duster rather timidly. In fact she never really removed the dust, she merely rearranged it.

The house was looking decidedly shabby. Because of Meg's protracted illness, we hadn't looked after it the way we should have done. Spring was in the air and the dark curtains gave the house a distinctly sinister appearance. Also, my garden was in peril. Oh, I had a gardener, an elderly gentleman who charged me the earth for plucking a clump of groundsel. He seemed strangely indifferent as the grass on the lawns crept slowly past his waist. If I mentioned the word 'lawnmower' he would turn quite pale, clutch his chest and mutter 'angina'. Now, when Meg was alive the old devil had done what he was told, if the wife had said 'Plant these dog roses', by God he did, and I began to realise what running a house meant.

As a widower, everybody took advantage of me.... The plumber for instance. Once, when we had a burst pipe, Meg had phoned him up to come round immediately. He had hummed and hawed and tried to put her off, but she was adamant and he duly arrived. Now I had reason to ask him to call and mend a washer on a tap, you would have thought I was telephoning a Harley

Street specialist! First of all, his wife said she would have to look through his appointment book – that took ten minutes and a great deal of tutting. Eventually she put me on to the Great Man and he condescended to consider me in three days' time.

I had to come to grips with door to door salesmen who promised me paradise if I purchased a can of their wonder polish; a double glazing whizz kid came at least twice a week then stayed on the doorstep for an hour. Religious nuts were a constant factor – Mormons, Jehovah's Witnesses by the battalion dragging peculiar converts with them, fussy female Methodists selling me endless bundles of raffle tickets, and one loon who kept popping up trying to get me to buy a piece of wood from the Cross of Christ. Never before had I understood half the problems a housewife has to contend with. Then in my loneliness, I made the fatal mistake of inviting a neighbour in for a coffee. Over that cup of coffee came a kindly but rigid determination to oversee life. She started to bring round a tray upon which was a hot meal for the kids and me. When I threw a bit of it to our dog, he spent an hour with a paw down his throat. Next she fixed me up with a window cleaner who must have spent years in the Navy washing portholes, never once did he complete a full pane. I started hiding under the settee when she rang the bell, but that didn't deter her, on the doorstep she'd leave a homemade hot-pot, a pudding or a baked fish dish which was so appalling the dog left home. It took my eldest daughter to open the door to her one day whilst I cowered on the floor of the lounge, to tell her straight that she appreciated what she had done but thank you, we could manage. The good lady sniffed audibly and took her pots back.

* * *

Julie returned to her nursing, Stuart had a job as a motor mechanic, and Pamela left school and went to work with the Blackpool Tourist Board.

I badly needed to get back to work; I simply wasn't strong enough to cope with running a home, so in May I toured a show around the smaller resorts and did fairly good business. Two of the kids were at home looking after things. God only knows what they got up to in my absence, and I thought it prudent to remain in ignorance.

And another thing – widowed ladies had started beaming at me and offering me a cuppa in their homes. At first I thought they were just being friendly – until one bright-blue-rinsed predator put her hand on my thigh and boomed: 'A man wasn't meant to be alone.'

I received letters from women who made it quite clear what their motives were, and although I found a lot of it amusing, it also saddened me to think how much loneliness there is in the world. The thought of ever getting married again never entered my head; I'd had the good fortune of knowing a fine woman, I would never find her like again in my lifetime.

For relaxation I used the bar of the St Ives Hotel and as always it was nice to chat with the beautiful Tracy. She was married with two children, and very popular with everybody who used the hotel. What chance would I have had with her, even if I'd wanted to get to know her better?

Tracy

The guests at the St Ives Hotel saw the little fat man drinking heavily as he sat at the bar, exchanging jokes with other drinkers who laughed loudly at his silly stories, especially the one about the man who looked into the shaving mirror and saw a small tree growing on his cheekbone. He wiped some shaving soap off his chin and saw a little stream running from his ear to his mouth, and halfway down the stream was a bridge with a milkmaid on it, and the sun on the man's forehead was shining down on to a basket of flowers that the milkmaid was carrying towards a cottage nestling under his lip.

The man went to see the doctor and the doctor said: 'Don't worry over it ... it's a beauty spot.'

The guests saw the other drinkers slap the little fat man on his shoulder – but what they didn't see was the way the little man looked at the lovely young woman behind the bar.

It was now six months since Meg had passed away, and I was just about feeling my feet again.

I went out a lot and once or twice in a drunken stupor I would go out with a woman then instantly regret it before anything came of it. I couldn't forget Meg.... But sometimes I would think of Tracy behind the bar, with her broad smile.... I was confused and diving into a well of self-imposed depression again. The answer was to work, and I shot off to London to finish off a series of *Blankety Blank*.

Even in London Meg was still with me. She had been so well liked and loved, people simply couldn't help talking about her. Yes, it was nice, we had been a team, Meg and I. We had been one of show business's most respected couples ... but that was now in the past.

When one partner in a marriage is left on his or her own, no matter how kind people are towards you, all they talk about is the past – and you find yourself relegated to that past along with your partner. It's as if they cannot see you having a separate future. It was that attitude that took me to Meg's graveside, where I spoke about my feelings to her photograph on the headstone.

I was fifty-one years of age, not in the best of physical shape, but none too bad considering the life I'd led. Should I now allow the years to slide by and content myself with watching the children find themselves, or should I look to my life and salvage something worthwhile from it?

I had talent, I could make people laugh, couldn't I? I couldn't believe that God had put us on this earth to wallow in what used to be, rather than to strive for a future that might be.... I talked and talked to Meg, and the comfort I received in return only confirmed my belief that death is not final, it is merely a transition.

I was approached by the *Daily Mirror* for an interview about life without Meg, and to write a three-part article. I agreed on condition that I had copy approval before publication and that I was to be paid the sum of twenty-five thousand pounds, which would go to Christie's Hospital for any equipment they might need. The newspaper agreed, and a contract was signed.

Meanwhile I found myself spending more and more time in the St Ives Hotel. It was no good kidding myself, I was drawn to Tracy, mainly because she was a sympathetic listener and she seemed to care. She herself, I discovered, had experienced many tragedies. She had lost both her parents; her mother from cancer and her father in a car accident. She was about to give birth to her son, Richard, when the police came to tell her that her father was dead. At the time she was alone, still mourning her mother, who'd been dead only a few months. She had nearly lost her young son when he was terribly scalded in a household accident, and soon afterwards she herself had nearly died of peritonitis.

That summer, I opened in Ray Cooney's farce, *Run For Your Wife* at the Grand Theatre, Blackpool. It had an excellent cast: Eric Sykes, Jan Hunt, Peter Goodwright, Paul Toothill and Jilly Foote. Bookings were good and we were all set for a fifteen-week run.

Together with Hilary Bonner, a friend who was a feature writer on the *Daily Mirror*, I worked on the article about life without Meg, and we were both pleased with it. One night, my agent rang to say that another newspaper, a Sunday publication, wanted to do a feature on my latest books, *A Time Before Genesis* and *A Clown Too Many.* I agreed to see the reporter – quite an affable chap – and we sat in my dressing-room and talked about the books. Only once did he ask me how things were now that I was alone. I replied 'Fine' and that was that ... or so I thought. But then an article appeared in this Sunday newspaper about life without Meg – virtually the same article that was intended for the *Daily Mirror*. A tearful Hilary Bonner rang me. Apparently she knew the man who'd interviewed me; he'd put together the free two-page spread with information dug out of the archives. I was desolate, it looked as if Christie's wouldn't get the money now. Fortunately, I hadn't reckoned with my agents' experience with this sort of situation: the *Mirror* held to the contract and I received a cheque for twenty-five thousand pounds made out to Christie's Hospital, Manchester. Now came the part I was looking forward to.

I telephoned the hospital and spoke to the head administrator. The conversation went something along the lines of:

ME: 'Oh hello, my name is Dawson, Les Dawson, my wife was under your care for cancer.'

HIM: 'Yes, I know, we were all terribly sorry, Mr Dawson, or may I call you Les?'

ME: 'Sure. The reason I'm ringing you is to find out if a donation would be of any help to you.'

HIM: 'Oh yes, we're grateful for anything we can get, no matter how small.'

ME: 'Is there anything in particular that you need desperately?'

HIM: 'Well, yes, we need equipment for the children's cancer ward, and we need it badly.'

This was the moment I'd been waiting for.

ME: 'Would twenty-five thousand pounds be any use to you?'

There was the longest silence ever on a telephone, then I heard a sharp intake of breath on the other end of the line, and a strangled: 'Oh yes, yes.'

'Well, there will be a cheque in the post to you tonight for that amount.'

The administrator said, 'Why don't we have a presentation ceremony?'

'No,' I said. 'All I ask is that on whatever equipment you buy, just put an inscription saying "In loving memory of Meg Dawson".'

The voice on the other end said: 'Be assured that will be done, and many many thanks.... Oh, there's just one thing I'd like to add.'

'What's that?' I asked.

'... God bless you.'

It's an old cliché that tells us 'It's better to give than to receive'. Well, I'm here to tell you how very true that is.

I sat at Meg's grave and a soft breeze, warm and indolent, brushed the evening shadows around me as I talked to her headstone, and I knew that she would have been highly pleased with what I'd managed to do.

Meanwhile, our play was doing enormous business whilst other shows in the resort were having a rough time of it ... we were taking all the money.

With someone as funny and experienced as Eric Sykes alongside me on stage, I had to work twice as hard to keep up with him. He was such an inventive comedian, and on many occasions the show would overrun by an hour! Much to the delight of the holiday audiences, I hasten to add.

Whilst in Blackpool, I was asked to switch on the Illuminations. It is a great honour to be invited to do this, and to a backstreet kid like myself, it was the apex of my career. I brought the entire cast on to the podium with me alongside the glittering array of officials and sponsors. Talbot Square was packed with thousands of people, and from their throats came a roar that rent the warm September night. Hundreds of sparkling arc lamps focus on to the staging area; the big switch stands before me; television cameras are set to record the big event; it is a thrilling moment as I depress the lever – and suddenly it is a make-believe world and one is a child again as the shimmering ranks of lights spark into animation along the length of the promenade, and the soaring steel of the Tower is clothed in a million moons.... The Blackpool Illuminations are on for another year, and there is no sight to equal it. Children's faces reflect the wonder of it all and the grown-ups, too, are breathless.

There is music and champagne and laughter and all the meaner aspects of life are forgotten, if only for one magical night.

I'd asked Tracy to come along but she had declined, and yet again I asked myself, what had I done that for?

Actually, I had suggested that we might see each other from time to time, just as two people who had shared tragedies together, nothing else ... but secretly I had to ask myself if I was merely kidding myself and ignoring my real feelings.

After the show I would go straight to the hotel and talk to her, and watch her deftly tend to her customers, and always I saw the genuine smile and the concern in her big eyes. She started to scold me about the amount of whisky I was consuming and I decided to pull myself away from the habit.... But why? What had I got to look forward to?

I should have known that someone was drawing the

strings of destiny together.... Summer drew to a close and the last-night party was behind me and the future ahead.

I did some television appearances, but nothing auspicious, and soon it was pantomime again ... so soon, so short the years.

I found myself spending more time than ever at the St Ives. I kept telling myself that it was the company that gathered there that was the attraction, it was a break for me to get out of the house where the memories still hung like ghostly curtains, for let's face it, despite being surrounded by a wonderful cast and friends I was desperately lonely. When the spotlight is turned off, you really are on your own.

My attention was forever drawn to the lovely lass behind the bar ... Tracy. Quite by accident I discovered from one of her colleagues that despite the wide attractive smile and the vivacious manner, she was not very happily married. I pushed her image from my mind and concentrated on drinking. OK, I reasoned with myself, the girl had a personality that kept me spellbound, but she was another man's wife, and there was no way that I intended to make matters worse for her and her children, even supposing that she might welcome my advances, which I doubted very much.

There was, of course, an even greater reason for dismissing her from my thoughts ... the age difference.

There were seventeen years between us; a chasm that could not be easily bridged.

I stopped going to the hotel and went drinking elsewhere.

The house was still an empty memory although the pain wasn't as bad now. It did help such a lot to be able to sit at Meg's grave and discuss my innermost thoughts with her. Nine long months had faded into the infinite since I'd laid her to rest, and self-pity was beginning to ravage me.... I had to start living again, if not for my sake then for Julie, Pamela and Stuart. I had to hold the family together.

About this time, a Doctor Peter Isaacs approached me to enlist my support for an appeal to raise money for a scanner machine for Blackpool's main hospital, Victoria.

It was such a worthy and necessary scheme that I didn't hesitate to join forces with him. Don't get me wrong, I am not a Do Gooder in any shape or form; I abhor and mistrust most charities, especially when there are big sums in evidence; also I firmly believe that we each pay enough in taxes for all the less fortunate members of our society to be taken care of. It's my belief that the more we do for charities, the less the ruling government is willing to do, so I am not a 'charity' person. However, Blackpool is regarded so much as simply a playground that many people in authority seem not to realise that it has a large population who work there and live there and die there.

Peter and I launched the Scanner Appeal and went to pubs, clubs and old folk's homes – where wonderful old ladies received a tonic to their lives by knitting tea cosies which we sold at an enormous profit at jumble sales, bring and buys, car boot sales.... We knocked piles of pennies down in the pubs, we begged, cajoled, pillaged and plundered all and sundry in order to reach our goal, which was to take nearly two years to attain.

It was costing me a fortune in taxis. Obviously I couldn't risk driving myself to all the venues because the amount of alcohol I was imbibing would have sent the breathaliser kit into Technicolor.

One night I was asked to go to the St Ives Hotel because

I made my pilgrimage to the grave and gave Meg a full report on the state of the kids and show business. It must have given a lot of people a shock to see a middle-aged, frumpish-looking man sitting by a headstone talking to himself! In fact, on one occasion, an elderly lady stooping at a grave quite close to Meg's, heard me chattering away to myself. She gave forth with a little shriek, crossed herself, and galloped wildly away in the direction of a grotto. But as I've said before, talking aloud certainly helped me overcome the loneliness that only someone who has lost their life's mate can fully understand.

Guilt is an emotion that destroys your peace of mind.... Could you have done more to lengthen the lost one's life? Whilst he or she was alive, were you a good partner? Did you give them all the love you had? I found myself feeling guilty about the weeks I'd spent away from home whilst trying to make a career. Gloomily I would recall our heated exchanges when I arrived home after an engagement feeling alienated from the rest of the family. She would storm that whilst I was away she had had to be all things – mother, transport chief, nurse, father, philosopher, teacher and playmate.... She would say: 'I know you work hard for us, but at least you get to meet different people ... apart from taking and picking up the kids from school, the kitchen window is my world.'

I would remember, and wish I could but see her once again to tell her how I regretted my thirst for ambition and how I wished now that all the days and nights we had spent apart could be brought back and relived.

I saw Tracy again in the hotel and we smiled and nodded to each other. I tried to avoid getting into a conversation with her but I couldn't stop looking at her.... It was getting ridiculous and noticeable and I felt foolish and inept.

The kids were peering at me as if they'd noticed some dramatic change in my behaviour.

I had started bathing more often which profoundly shocked them! Although my hair was thinning and receding, I spent more time pushing little waves into it and keeping it trimmed . . . I was acting like a love-sick bloody kid. . .

The daft part of all this, of course, was that not once had Tracy indicated any romantic interest in me whatsoever . . . she had merely been friendly, someone with a very nice shoulder to cry on.

Before I left for Birmingham, we met in the hotel and all the things I wanted to say evaporated as I looked at her. . . . She looked bewildered when I gulped down my drink and shrugged a passage through the crowded inn. . . . I drove to the furthest point of St Annes Bay, and sat smoking cigarette after cigarette as I watched the flickering lights of Southport illuminating the night sky. Over and over again I tormented myself with two burning issues: the age difference – a problem that wouldn't go away, and the seeming disloyalty of having feelings for another woman when my dear wife had been dead only ten months. The stupid thing was that all this was in my mind, and Tracy hadn't said a word about how she felt – that's assuming, of course, she felt anything for me other than sympathy.

I revved up the car and cruised home. Tomorrow I would be off to Birmingham and work would be the best tonic for my jaded spirits.

I threw myself into bed and tried to sleep, but that soothing balm evaded me. Suddenly the telephone jangled. When I picked up the receiver, my heart stopped . . . the call was from Tracy. 'Are you all right?' she inquired in that breathy voice.

I gabbled something, God knows what, but I must have sounded like a teenager on his first date.

'Will you let me know how you are when you go away for the pantomime?' She managed to get a word in edgeways.

'I'm going to miss you, Tracy,' I said lamely.

There was a long pause, then words came across the void that sent my heart tap dancing.

'I'm going to miss you as well ... Les.' With that she put the receiver down.

We had a hectic schedule, in old Brum ... television interviews, personal appearances for publicity, radio shots and the harsh grind of rehearsals that eventually led to the opening night.

The show went extremely well and the first thing I did after it was over was – surprise surprise – to phone Tracy.

It was a joy to hear her voice again. Our telephone chats became a legend with the cast and a great boost to British Telecom's profits.... As soon as the curtain dropped, I would be off to the Albany Hotel and straight on to the telephone, and Tracy and I gossiped away like fishwives – not romantic things, just general topics – and hopefully I made her laugh, because she did mention that she was unhappy with her domestic affairs.

Christmas came and went, and at a company party on New Year's Eve I excelled myself: I phoned Tracy and we spent five hours talking ... five hours of utter contentment, at least for me.

The cast were very aware of my mood changes, and my dear friend Mo, who was the first Roly Poly, bluntly asked me what was wrong. I told her how I was frightened of my feelings for a woman who up to now had shown little interest of a romantic nature in me. I babbled on about my guilt for having such feelings so soon after Meg's death, and it was that little bundle of energy, Mighty Mo, who finally made me see sense:

'What the hell are you worrying about, lad?' she said genially. 'Everybody knows how much you loved Meg, and she'd be the first to wish you all the luck in the world if you found a new love in your life. Meg wasn't the sort of woman who would expect you to stay alone for the rest of your life. From what you've told me, I reckon this Tracy likes you a lot more than you realise.'

She turned to leave the dressing-room. 'But Mo,' I whispered, 'it can't be right, can it? Meg's not been dead twelve months yet.... Suppose anything did come of it, what would the kids and other people say?'

She looked at me with a glance that was a wee bit scornful.

'There is no time limit on mourning, lad. If God has decided to find someone else for you to love, thank him. As for the children, well, if they love you they'll want you to be happy, won't they?'

I nodded dumbly.

'As for what other people think, it's your life not theirs.... It's a tribute to the happiness you had with Meg that you want to rekindle the same love with Tracy.... Give the lass a ring, and do it sharp.' With that parting shot she went on stage.

I telephoned Tracy and said quietly and simply: 'I love you.'

She caught her breath on the other end of the line. 'I love you as well, darling.'

I couldn't wait for the end of the pantomime now! Mark you, conducting a romance by telephone wasn't always happy. Frustration and jealousy would cause us both to have blazing rows, one in particular I recall....

We had been quite chummy on the line after one show – we'd spoken for about fifteen minutes then said our goodnights. I was in a euphoric mood. I left the theatre and tripped over to the hotel, where instead of going to bed I joined some of the cast in the bar, and Tommy Steele, who was appearing at the Hippodrome Birmingham for the season, joined us. The phone rang in the bar ... it was my Divinity, Tracy. 'Hello darling,' I warbled.

'Just what the hell are you doing in the bar?' She raved on and on. I got angry, and heads turned towards where I was standing, quivering with rage and shouting back at her. We both slammed down the receivers at the same time and I strode back to the party and drank long and deep.... To hell with her.

There was no communication from her the next day nor did I phone her. During the interval of the second house of the panto that night, she rang the dressing-room. My heart soared – she was about to apologise, wasn't she? I would be magnanimous, of course, and forgive the sweet wren....

Tracy said: 'Don't you ever phone me again.'

Goodbye romance, hello unwanted bachelorhood. I stalked into the private theatre bar and made them open up. 'Drinks all round,' I boomed to the curious cast. 'You see before you a man scorned, a man bereft of love. From this day forward, once a month a lady of my choice will ease my loins! Not for me the bondage of one woman's love – for me, only the pit of selfish desire, and ego doth drive me on.' John Nettles raised his pint and roared his approval. At that moment, the stage door-keeper poked his head into the noisy, smoke-filled bar and shouted in his rich Brummie accent: 'Phone call for Mr Dawson from someone called Tracy.'

I shot out of my seat like a startled fawn and broke all records to get to the phone.

'Hello?' I managed to stammer.

Tracy's breathless voice came along the line: 'Why didn't you call me back? We can be friends, can't we?'

'Oh yes, yes, we can,' I panted. Although I would have preferred her to say she loved me passionately, I was content with her friendship . . . in any case, I had no right to expect anything more.

I went back to my beer and John eyed me with suspicion but said nothing. I told Mo that we were just going to be friends and she smiled knowingly.

At last I knew where I stood. I had been foolish to allow myself to forget my loneliness in secret dreams of a woman I could never have; now I would get on with my life without any more thoughts of romance.

In any case, it was just as well. She was married, albeit not happily, but at least I wasn't responsible for that as both she and her friends had told me that the marriage hadn't been right for a long time. She had her two children and I had mine . . . our two lives were not destined to conjoin.

The run of *Babes in the Wood* ground on to its conclusion and frankly I was knackered. . . . Fourteen weeks, twice nightly, takes an enormous amount of stamina, and I needed a rest. I didn't see Tracy for a month. I kept myself busy at home writing magazine articles and attempting to write a new book. There were also a few engagements I'd agreed to do, golf pro-celebrity occasions that I hosted for charity, radio interviews, and a commercial for an organ and piano manufacturer, which didn't pay a lot but was fun to do. This led to a poster advertisement for Heineken, in which I was shown dressed as Ada drinking from a pint pot. The last frame showed me with a paper bag over my head, and the caption read: '... Refreshes the parts other beers cannot reach'....

I thought of Tracy quite often and I was glad that our relationship had been purely platonic, otherwise I think I would have gone potty.

The year strode on; March gave way to a skittish April and I was back televising *Blankety Blank* once more. The show never failed to amaze me: its popularity never seemed to wane and it looked as if it would be on the screens forever.

I called into the St Ives to see a friend, and there was Tracy, beaming and vivacious as ever.... I nodded to her and she seemed pleased to see me, but I kept a low profile. I didn't want to appear to moon over her; in any case she was surrounded by hearty customers, all of whom were vying for her attention. I looked at myself in a mirror and I didn't like what I saw – a woman's man I wasn't.

Then something occurred that made me hopeful that my life wasn't just meant to grind joylessly on into oblivion. Rummaging through my suits to make sure no money was secreted in them, prior to having them dry-cleaned, I chanced upon a letter that was still in its envelope.

Curious, I sat on the edge of the bed and glanced through it... baffled at first, but then the penny dropped. I recalled the stage door-keeper handing me the letter saying that it had been left by an elderly lady who claimed to be a spiritualist specialising in automatic writing. She had told him that what was written on the paper had been guided by Meg's hand. As I sat on the bed, all the memories flooded back and the tears came.

Eventually I read the letter. Frankly, a lot of it didn't make sense, but the one indisputable fact was that the letter was written in Meg's handwriting. The slant of the sentences, the quirks of certain letters .... One snatch of a sentence: 'need to find the bag'. Another: 'Les.... Must watch his chest,' Bits and pieces.... 'Be happy, find someone to care.'

I have to say that I keep an open mind on the paranormal.

The letter made me wonder if the outer limit of our solar system is not one vast telephone exchange.... Silly idea? Well, science tells us that sounds never really fade into nothingness; if I tap a pencil, for instance, on a table top, the sound will be sharp and loud but will then dissipate from my hearing – but that does not mean the sound has died out... it has merely gone from my earshot into the ether, where it will stay. Sounds are like ripples on a pond: without the banks to contain them, they would go on for ever.

In that strange, disjointed astral letter was a warning of something to come much later on.... A portent....

Meanwhile, life in the here and now had to go on. I had to look after my two teenage kids – no easy task! My cooking wasn't getting any better, and they were eating more junk food than ever. As for myself, I seemed to exist on strong drink and pies, which caused my weight to balloon into obesity.

I still went for my talks with Meg, but I think if she could have replied she would have told me to bugger off, I was so maudlin.

I heard that Tracy and her family were going on holiday together, which seemed to indicate that they were patching their marriage up.

One or two women were showing an interest in me – God knows why, I can only assume they were part-time workers for the Samaritans. I dated one lady who appeared normal on the surface but who had one burning ambition, I discovered: to drink the planet dry. Her behaviour before alcohol wasn't too bad, but after a bout with the demon drink she became Mr Hyde. Once she even tried to take her clothes off on the prom.

Another lady, introduced to me by a friend, steered me to the window of a large furnishing store and cooed: 'Isn't that bedroom suite...?' I fled; I'd only met the lady an hour or two before and already it appeared that she had matrimony on her mind.

I'd never realised how vulnerable a lonely man can be. Some men are natural loners ... believe me, I wasn't. I liked having a woman around and all too easily I made myself the prey of calculating females.

One night, feeling a trifle down in spirits and determined to top up with the other kind, I ventured to see some friends in the St Ives. I couldn't believe my eyes: Tracy was behind the bar – she should have been away on holiday.

She told me that she hadn't wanted to go; despite the children, something had stopped her from going. I didn't pursue the subject, feeling instinctively that she was still upset.

A week later I saw her by accident in St Annes Square. She was pale and looked awful. I dashed over to her. 'Hi Tracy, what's the matter?' I said.

She looked at me helplessly. Without speaking she drew an official-looking document from her handbag and handed it to me. It was a divorce petition from her husband.

I went to Meg's grave and I told her what had transpired. 'I loved you, Meg, you know that, don't you?' I whispered to the headstone. 'Now there's this young woman, a lot younger than me, but I just know that we could be happy together.... We've both been unhappy – please, Meg, tell me that I have your blessing to love someone again ... please.'

It was quiet in the graveyard and only the murmur of a tired breeze disturbed the silence, but on that breeze, and lingering around Meg's grave, I swear I caught the scent of freesias. Meg's favourite flower. Was she watching me? Was her spirit energy there?

Tracy moved into a flat in the hotel where she worked and I prepared to leave for the tour of *Run For Your Wife*. What time we had we spent together either driving aimlessly in the car, munching Kentucky fried chicken, and acting like calf-lovers all over again, or walking along the beach by moonlight. I was head over heels in love. After playing Plymouth, Tracy agreed to spend the week in Bath with me and Pamela.

At this juncture I have to own up to a certain cowardice in breaking the news to my three children, all of whom were quite old enough to be consulted, I must add. On the couple of occasions when Tracy had been to my house, I had merely introduced her in a very off-hand manner to Julie, Stuart and Pamela. Never once had I intimated that our relationship was more than friendship; I didn't want to upset them because I knew they were still grieving for their mother. Certainly they had received Tracy warmly enough, but they remained more than a little wary of her. What was I to say? That I was in love with another woman when their mother had only been gone eighteen months?

And so I opted for treating my relationship with Tracy as just a pal's act. It was to take the children a long time to come to grips with their father falling for another woman.... When they did, they gave me a telling off for not being honest with them at the time.

Having Tracy around was wonderful and our stay in

Bath helped her to overcome her depression at the impending divorce. From Bath, we played Nottingham (Theatre Royal), Lincoln, Manchester, Reading (the Hexagon) and then the old Theatre Royal at Brighton – a week of pure delight. What a lovely old traditional place to perform in!

The long haul to Darlington, too, was well worth the trek, for the Civic Theatre in that old railway town is quite superb, and there was the bonus of staying in a baronial suite in a 12th-century castle that reeked of the past – and my ninety-per cent proof breath.

Although no great traveller, I adore touring. It's a chance to see what a varied country we live in and the differences to be found in the people within relatively short distances. From Darlington to Norwich and from Norwich to Dartford, we played to capacity houses, and with Tracy at my side, my happiness knew no bounds.

In September I was invited to play golf in the Howard Keel Pro-Celebrity tournament. Unfortunately, being in transit between theatre dates, I couldn't play in the actual competition, but I was able to attend the dinner. I asked Tracy to go with me, but first I cleared it with her solicitor who said there was absolutely no reason why she should not accompany me as she was now on the verge of divorce.

I felt so proud showing off my new love, but I was also worried what people's attitude would be, for many of the stars attending the ball that night had known Meg for years and she had been adored by so many in the business. But it had to be faced.

As soon as my fellow guests saw Tracy, they melted, as I had done, under her radiant charm. I need not have worried after all.

Love Under Scrutiny

The other revellers at the Howard Keel Golf Classic Dinner looked curiously at the fat little man with the Junoesque beauty at his side. They saw them hold hands tightly throughout the evening, and he seemed to make her laugh a lot.

Their table companions joined in the laughter when he told the joke about the old man sitting on a wall in the street, crying his eyes out.

'What's the matter?' asked a passer-by. 'Are you all alone in the world, old chap?'

The old man shook his head.

'You seem to be very unhappy,' said the passer-by.

The old man blew his nose and replied: 'I'm the happiest man in the world. I'm ninety-seven, married to a twenty-five year-old ex-beauty queen who is also a Cordon Bleu cook. We have sex three times a day and she's bought me a Rolls Royce for my birthday.'

The passer-by said angrily, 'Then what the bloody hell are you crying for?'

And the old man said, 'I can't remember where I live.'

What the fat little man didn't see was a furtive figure snatching a photograph of him and the blonde beauty at his side. . . .

* * *

I awoke on Monday morning with a gnome tapping out a tattoo on my head. I turned over but the tapping wouldn't go away. I sat up and the tapping went on, but it wasn't coming from the gnome's hammer, it was coming from downstairs. Somebody was knocking on my back door.

I squinted at the clock. Eight-thirty am. Who could it be? The tapping was now beginning to irritate me. I groaned to my unsteady feet, donned my moth-chewed dressing-gown and lurched down the stairs. The tapping was more insistent. 'For the love of Christ,' I yelled, 'I'm coming....'

I shuffled into the kitchen and banged into the spin-drier in the wash-house. Peering through the glass panels of the back door I saw the shapes of two men.

Gingerly I opened the door a crack and was about to scream 'I don't want to be a Jehovah's Witness', when a voice from the other side shouted: 'Morning, Les, have you got a minute? It's —— from the *Daily* —.'

Newspaper reporters at this time? Some bugger big must have cashed his Giro in, I thought, as I opened the door.

'What can I do for you, chaps?' I said, not suspecting a thing.

One of the heavily overcoated gentlemen held out a newspaper photograph of Tracy and myself at the Howard Keel ball.

'Who is she, Les?' he asked, and before I could answer, his friend held out a copy of another tabloid, and there for all the world to see was the same photograph with the caption: 'Who is the mystery blonde in Les's life?'

The report went on to make the point that I'd only recently lost Meg and here I was, a respected family man, already frolicking with another woman....

The one thing that I had feared had happened. I tried to make light of it. 'She's just a friend, fellers,' I smiled. Why had this been raked up? I smelt a bad time ahead with the press.

'Is she married, Les?' the bigger of the two men smirked.

I held on to my temper. It's no use letting reporters like this get to you, it only serves to give a piece of trivia more substance than it deserves.

'I don't know, chaps. She's just a lady I took to a dance, that's all,' I lied through my fillings.

On and on they probed. I fended them off with bad jokes; finally I ran out of patience and slammed the door on them.

I telephoned Tracy to tell her the news that our relationship had been leaked to the press, and naturally the poor lass cried in horror. For somebody who has never been exposed to the glare of publicity, it can be a terrible experience, and I find this type of sensationalist journalism an indictment of the grotesque society we've built for ourselves. When you think that half the planet's population is dying of hunger or disease, that millions of people live a hand to mouth existence, yet what makes headlines? A Northern comedian who lost his wife to cancer and has somehow managed to find a new love to share his life.

That morning the phone never stopped ringing. Was it true? Had I found another woman? Over and over I heard the same banal questions.

I telephoned Tracy again and reminded her that she hadn't done anything wrong. I had taken her as my guest to the Howard Keel gala dinner with the full blessing of her solicitor. Despite the threatened squall of sensational stories, she could hold her head high . . . and stop thinking that we were a sort of suburban Bonnie and Clyde.

To my horror, a local radio station crooned out the story of 'Les and his mystery blonde', ending with 'Do you know who she is? If you think you do, give us a ring.' Carte blanche for every crackpot north of the Wash to jam the airways!

As I went round the shops I was aware of much staring and nudging – however this was tempered by a lot of encouraging smiles.

Early Monday morning I had tried to drive to Bradford, and a black saloon that had been parked by the side of my garden wall slid into gear and followed me all the way from my home, across the M62 motorway, to the doors of the theatre, where two shifty, ill-kempt men – obviously press – were trying to make themselves invisible at the stage door entrance. The Big Heat was on. The theatre publicity lady had a Bradford newspaper showing yours truly on the front page, and as usual it was the most unflattering photograph possible. . . . I looked evil and quite pissed, and my eyes glared from the photograph like those of an oversexed ferret.

I warned the theatre manager and the company manager to watch out for the newshounds, and went ahead with the rehearsal, putting the other business out of my head . . . for the time being. The cast – Peter Goodwright, Jilly Foote, Anna Dawson and her husband John Boulter, Brian Cant and Brian Godfrey – were marvellous. They had met Tracy and liked her, and of course they had known of my unhappiness. Now they shielded me from the prying noses of the tabloid legions, who by this time were encircling the theatre. I was damned if I'd make any statement yet.

Apart from being kind and comradely, the cast were

also highly talented, and our opening night in Bradford was a resounding success. We took five long curtain calls; nobody in the audience heckled me about Tracy. There was a solid ring of reporters around the Alhambra, so after the first-night party, Jilly Foote donned large dark glasses and strutted out of the stage door and into the heaving mêlée of reporters and fans waiting for autographs. The press thought she was Tracy and she pretended she was, which gave me a chance to be smuggled out another way. The management pushed me into a waiting car and off we sped to Lancashire ... silently pursued by the black limousine.

As soon as I arrived home, I ran the gauntlet of some newsmen at the gate, and telephoned Tracy at her flat... then almost wished I hadn't, because the press had found out her identity, and the hotel where she worked was now under siege. I could tell by her voice that she was frightened. I hadn't got the heart to tell her that it was going to get considerably worse. The house was empty. My son was out with a girlfriend and Pamela, who was my dresser in the show, had stayed on in Bradford at my request. I didn't want the press to start questioning her at this stage of the drama.

Although I was replete with the fiery spirit, I still managed to find accommodation for another few large whiskies, and then staggered around the house talking loudly to no one, uttering audible profanities to the hacks outside and feeling generally sorry for myself. What sort of bloody future lay ahead? I was experiencing such guilt, I cried out for Meg ... and then a sense of peace came over me when I smelt the heady perfume that suddenly hung in the air. It was the smell of freesias.

I slept in late and ignored the never-ending jangling of the telephone. I made myself coffee and glanced at the newspaper headlines. Normally I only bought one particular newspaper, and that was just for the crossword in it, but my local newsagent always scanned the papers in case there was anything in about me, and he'd send along anything relevant for me to peruse. He'd had a field day with the morning editions.... I was plastered on the front pages, the middle pages; there were articles wishing me all the happiness in the world, as well as one calling me a dirty old man.

Headlines screamed at me that Tuesday morning; some said I was a wife stealer, others noted that Meg hadn't been dead all that long and quite a few couldn't resist the usage of the word Barmaid when they ranted on about Tracy. What was once considered a respectable occupation, now appeared as if it was merely a job for busty sluts; the fact that Tracy was a trained hotelier had been totally ignored by the hacks, it made Tracy look and sound tarnished. I have never forgiven the tabloids for that.

Amongst the printed idiocy there were a couple of items that made me chuckle, I must confess. Some cartoons made me howl and one tongue-in-cheek article called me an 'off the wall Casanova'.

It really was all very ridiculous. My self-control was wearing a bit thin when I attempted to go outside the house and was greeted with a positive barrage of flashes, blinding me into retreat.

Poor Tracy was practically a prisoner in her hotel flat, and other employees stood on sentry duty to stave off the press.

It was quite obvious that something had to be done otherwise I could foresee the weekend's papers having a ball at our expense. There were eight reporters standing at the gates to my drive, and that wasn't counting the ones who hung like figs up the trees with telescopic lenses on their Japanese cameras.... It was all worthy of a Mack Sennett farce. All it needed now was the arrival of Buster Keaton to complete the picture. Once or twice I tried to chat to them; after all, I knew quite a lot of them. I wouldn't give any statement, I just asked them what they thought the scandal was, if any? Naturally they couldn't tell me because there wasn't one and there never had been.

I was haunted by the thought that Meg hadn't been given a decent period of mourning ... but how do you avoid love when you need it to exist?

I had to fight to leave the house and drive off to the show in Bradford late that Tuesday afternoon, and sure enough, the black saloon was gliding behind me across the barren moors.

The stage door was awash with the eager scribes, and a brace of hefty security men flanked me into the theatre. I felt like Crippen stepping off the boat after his arrest. The manager came into my dressing-room looking more than a trifle distraught.

I paused in putting on my make-up. 'Look, I'm sorry about all this press nonsense, I know it's a damn nuisance and you may have a lot of people asking for their money back if they're offended by what they read.' He put his hand on my shoulder and said, 'Don't worry about the business, Les. I could sell the seats for twice as much and still not have enough room to pack them in!'

I felt mortified. I rang Tracy before the curtain went up, and she gasped out, 'I love you, Lumpy.'

Oh yes ... I must relate at this point that Tracy and I had nicknames for each other; she was Poo and, of course, I was Lumpy.... I know, I know, it's infantile, but when my children were small I used to tell them stories about

Lump the Elf and his pretty wife Poo the Pixie. As I've mentioned before, Tracy had a simplicity that brought out the child in me that refused to go when I became a man ... and thank God that child didn't go, because without the child within us we are forever lost.

It was so good to hear her voice over the phone; she was bearing up well despite the fact that the hotel was still under siege and she was a virtual prisoner.

With only a scant few minutes to go before the curtain went up on Act I, the telephone rang. I thought hopefully it might be Tracy ... it wasn't, and I was sorry that I'd answered it.

A few years before I had played a town in the Midlands – a very big town that gave me and the pantomime a warm welcome and capacity business. During the run there, the cast was looked after by a young girl, a very nice young lady. In retrospect I think I was too friendly with her, because I felt that she was looking upon me as if I were the father whom she had recently and tragically lost. She developed an infatuation, I think, and I didn't realise it at the time. I treated her like a daughter, and that was all.

It was she who had telephoned me that Tuesday night, very upset about Tracy and myself. She threatened to tell the newspapers that it should be her and not Tracy who was the new love of my life.... That was all I needed.

The curtain rose and the first act began. Suddenly, as I stood in the wings peering out at the capacity audience, a thunderbolt hit me. *Run For Your Wife* is all about infidelity, the press, and messy marriages.... I'd never thought about it before but now, with all the lurid headlines, it came as a bit of a shock. It was my entrance; I opened the door in the set and stood for a moment framed in the doorway. In every town and city we had played on the tour, my first entrance had been greeted with hearty applause. Tonight? Nothing. Just an intense silence. It threw me, and the good lines between Peter Goodwright and myself on this occasion were gleaning no laughs. The audience was waiting. We came to the part where my character (Stanley) cannot understand Peter's not wanting the newspapers to know about his heroism, because at this point in the play Stanley doesn't know that Peter is a bigamist! Now was the time to step out of character. . . .

ME: 'What's up, old son?'
PETER: 'You don't understand, Stanley.'
ME: 'No, I damn well don't, with all the rubbish printed in the papers today.' (At this point I stood and faced the audience.) 'And when it comes to rubbish in the papers, by hell I know what I'm talking about.'

The audience roared with laughter and there were shouts of 'Sod 'em . . . be happy,' and 'Good on you, Les.' It was like a tonic, all the tension drained away from me. . . .

'They've got me down as a cross between Bluebeard and a randy bull terrier.'

'The last woman I had on the side was a suffragette . . . and that's because she was chained to the railings.'

'Since the papers have been having a go at me, I keep dreaming that I'm playing cricket for England. A pal of mine said, "I thought you would have been dreaming about making love to a beautiful woman." I said, "What? And lose my chance to bat?"'

The audience loved the silly gags and it took a long time to get back into the play. I felt close to tears that night, it was wonderful to feel that ordinary people were on my side. What nobody knew was that only about forty minutes earlier, in the dressing-room before the play began, I had stared into the mirror and faced a moment of truth....

Many, many years ago I had been under contract to the great Max Wall. He had meant well enough but I was having a hard time in London. I'd been thrown out of my lodgings in Battersea and I'd spent some nights on a bench in Hyde Park, and I don't recommend it.

Occasionally Max would give me a fiver to get myself a cheap room. I eventually found one in an old house in Notting Hill Gate, a tiny, cramped attic with just a bed and a gas ring. Rent? Two pounds. Eagerly I took it.

Max Wall was the biggest comedy star of the day. He was playing Hymie, a leading character in a hit musical play called *The Pyjama Game* with Joy Nicols and Edmund Hockridge. Most performances I would sit in the great comedian's huge dressing-room doing odd jobs for him and listening to his stories and hopes for my future.

The world was his; I watched him in Regent Street surrounded by literally hundreds of fans; in cafés and restaurants people crowded around him, each one vying for his attention. Max Wall was at the very top of the theatrical tree, until he fell in love with a beauty queen over twenty years his junior. The newspapers and the morality of the day destroyed his career almost overnight. I watched him hold his head in despair and I could do nothing to comfort him.

People now crowded at the box office to get their money back. One night after the show, when Max and I came out of the stage door, people turned their backs on him. I remember there was a light drizzle falling, and it was misty. Max had had a lot to drink and I caught him as he stumbled against a wall. 'What have I done that is so terrible?' he whispered to me. 'All I did was to fall in love.'

Max went into oblivion after his affair with the young beauty queen was plastered on every billboard, and it would be many years before his greatness was once again acknowledged.

Now here I sat, at the top of my profession, facing the same situation. Would my love for Tracy destroy me?

Thankfully things had changed, and I reached out to an audience who understood that no man can be an island, and that happiness, when it comes, must be grasped tightly.

Wednesday's headlines became more bizarre ... on the front page of the paper was a photograph of the young lady whom I had apparently spurned. The caption read: 'I should have been the next Mrs Dawson.' That really hurt me because it was untrue, but the one that really made me consider homicide was: 'Spiritualist says, Carry on Bonking, Les.'

This newspaper had brought in a medium who was supposed to have got in touch with Meg's spirit, and my dead wife was supposed to have told her to tell me to 'carry on bonking'. Along with this garbage was a photograph of Meg's grave. The maudlin caption, supposedly spoken from beyond the grave, was so uncharacteristic of Meg that it was beyond belief – and beneath contempt.

It was high time to put the record straight about Tracy and myself. Hilary Bonner of the Mirror Group has never written anything spurious or untrue. Both Tracy and I look upon her as a friend, and it was to her that we turned to put an end to the ridiculous speculation. We gave her an exclusive and it was the best thing we could have done. Once the true story had been printed, the other newshounds vanished in a cloud of ink and by Friday it was some other poor bugger's turn to be castrated by the press.

Tracy and I still held sway in the newspapers but on a much happier note. We did interviews with magazines in which we declared our love for each other, and several newspapers printed follow-up stories after the furore died down. However, one paper would not leave well alone, and persisted in taking pot shots with a camera that looked so old it flared on magnesium. Their 'sleazy' pictures of the pair of us, were given ridiculous captions – one of Tracy, for instance, half vanishing into a supermarket, was trumpeted as: 'Les's lover on the town'. You'd have thought she was going for a binge in a Triad nightclub instead of popping in for a cabbage in Safeways.... One photograph of me was obviously taken through a hole in the garden fence. It showed me wearing shorts and nothing else plucking weeds from a stretch of rockery, and the headline read: 'The Loneliness of a Comic'.

Something had to be done about these clowns, and this realisation helped us to come to a major decision. By this time, Tracy's divorce had come through and she was now a free woman, but we had made no arrangements to live together and eventually get married. I still felt it was improper to wed so soon after my bereavement. There was also, of course, the fact that Tracy needed to get used to her new-found freedom and to make sure I was the right partner before going ahead.... At least, that's how I saw the situation.

Tracy could see her children whenever she wished, and she stayed on at the hotel. The need we felt for each other created many arguments, and we were never off the telephone to each other.

My children had now accepted her but they still blamed me for not being honest with them at the start, and they deserve an apology for that. We were in a state of emotional limbo – until the day Tracy rang me from her flat in near hysterics: 'Les – that awful newspaper wants me to talk about my marriage and tell them everything. . . . I can't leave the flat even; they've left a security man with me in case I try to contact another newspaper. Please, love, help me . . . I'm scared.'

I am not the stuff that heroes are moulded from, I'm too scared to fight and too fat to run, but Sir Galahad stirred in my bones. . . . The bastards! Now was the time for action.

I stopped at Meg's headstone on my way and poured out my feelings to her, and again I felt that her spirit energy was guiding me.

I drew up in the hotel's forecourt and walked to the door of Tracy's flat. I didn't ring the bell – I banged on the door.

A large man opened it and I brushed past him. He was most indignant at first but when he recognised me he smiled and said he was sorry.

'Tracy!' I shouted. She came out of the kitchen. Her soft eyes were clouded with sadness and she looked tired and drawn. My heart went out to her and I knew she was the one for me. 'Please God, make her feel the same about me,' I thought.

As though to allay my doubts Tracy ran towards me and embraced me. 'Les, I'm sorry, but I've had enough, love. Tell him to leave me alone, please.' She spoke urgently.

I pushed her gently away. I had made my decision. I turned to the man and said politely but very firmly: 'You can leave now, mate, because Tracy is going out of this flat and she is moving in with me. There will be no story, but you can tell your editor this. Tracy and I intend to marry as soon as possible, and we will announce our engagement this year. Now, my friend, go.'

I half expected some sort of argument but all he said was, 'Fine, and good luck to you both.'

Within two hours, Tracy was in my home and in my life forever.

It took her a while to recover from the experience of publicity. If you have never undergone the trial of exposure to the glare of public scrutiny then you cannot begin to understand how it can affect one's personality. For three days Tracy refused to leave the house. She believed that all eyes would be upon her, and I know that she felt the publicity had made her unclean in some way.

The oddest thing happened soon after. Several of the newspapers which had so hounded us now sent flowers and cards of good wishes! I forced Tracy to go out into the town and it helped her enormously when people smiled at us and wished us well. Never once did we encounter any hostility in the streets, although we did receive a mixed bag of mail. Some letters were so sick, the writers obviously needed some sort of treatment. Others carried religious messages; one from an amiable crackpot even suggested that Tracy was probably a Martian!

Most of the mail was nice and sincere; quite a lot came from men and women who had lost their partners and had never sought for another one. Now they regretted it. Loneliness in a crowded civilisation is a dreadful disease.

Being together was utter bliss and our love for each other seemed to bring out a glow in other people. It was like being born again. All the shadows in the house seemed to drift away and the light of happiness came in and created a warmth that Garth House had lost with so much sadness. With my encouragement, Tracy changed the furnishings and imposed her own personality on the décor of the house.

Two weeks later, the tour of *Run For Your Wife* ended and an exhausted band of players said their farewells – somewhat tearfully, because we had been together for so long we had become a family. So much had happened . . . I knew I'd made the right choice in Tracy, because at the foot of the stairs one night, the smell of freesias was almost overpowering. I knew then that I didn't need to talk to Meg's headstone any more, for it is my sincere belief that Meg led me to Tracy and gave my life a purpose again.

Work beckoned in the shape of a couple of cabaret functions for companies. Frankly, although the money is a big temptation, I'm not keen on performing at these do's. Too much drink is plied and with the best will in the world, businessmen en masse can be a difficult and noisy audience at times and it makes for hard work whilst performing for them. The nice thing now, of course, was that I no longer trotted all over the country on my own. I had Tracy at my side and it made all the difference: I no longer drank as heavily as of yore, and she frowned every time I lit up a cigarette, which was about fifty times a day. Someone cared about me. There can be no greater bliss.

Blankety Blank loomed on the hoizon, and it was off to London for the recordings.

Although the BBC provided a car and a driver to take us to London and back, it was nevertheless tiring and Tracy voiced her concern at our workload. On one trip to London, we saw two horrific accidents – one in which a woman was burning to death before our eyes. I had the shakes for the rest of the journey, knowing that at the other end, in a few short hours, I'd have to be funny....

Because of this we approached the BBC and told them that fatigue was becoming a major problem, and they agreed to fly us on the Manchester shuttle to London instead. This was a much better arrangement and our good friends at the St James Court Hotel gave us one of their apartments at a special rate. It was an ideal situation: fly down from the north on one day, do the programme, stay the night at the apartment and fly home the following day.

Despite flying instead of driving, it was still a pretty exhausting period, but our happiness was a stimulant and just being together without some idiot poking a camera in our faces was contentment enough.

Public opinion had swung in our favour when good and honest folk realised that ours was no fly-by-night affair, but a fine old full-blooded love story worthy of Mills and Boon. One thing that the glare of publicity had taught us was that it is an excellent method of finding out who your true friends are ... and we had a sort of spring-clean of fair-weather friends out of our lives, and felt the better for it.

Tracy was growing more and more confident with people with each passing day, and her bubbling personality and good looks won everyone over. I thoroughly enjoyed hearing the whispered comments from admiring males ... 'What does she see in him?' or (my favourite exclamation); 'Lucky little sod.' I must confess that in those early days I often pondered the same question ... what did she see in me? A much older man, raddled with excesses, and not very attractive to the female sex.... It certainly wasn't my wealth, because thanks to a lifetime of stupid over-indulgence and income taxes, I was far from being on Easy Street. God sparing me, I was destined to have to work for many years to attain even a passable level of comfort.

Yet I had the love of one of the finest women who ever lived ... Meg had been a wonderful wife, admired by many men, and sought by quite a few in marriage, and yet she'd chosen me. (The only physical difference between the Les Dawson then and the Les Dawson now was my waistline – that's one thing about ugliness, it endures through the years, unlike mere beauty that withers and dies.) And now I had gained the love of Tracy – at some stage I must have done something good in my life to deserve this!

Meg's mother had once loudly remarked: 'I don't know what she sees in that little bugger,' and now history was repeating itself. Tracy was hearing the same thing. The secret to a woman's heart is always to show her that you love her.... And remember, although there may not be many female comedians, women like laughter, and the man who can make them laugh has a great advantage.

In this day and age, the emphasis on sex is quite ridiculous; of course sex is important, but true love also includes a heady mixture of friendship, understanding and companionship. Compromise, despite what some say, is necessary for any marriage to work. It takes experience and discipline to be able to compromise, and it isn't taught in this competitive 'sod you' society.

I have never forgotten the words spoken by the Vicar of Wakefield in that marvellous novel of the same name.... 'I chose my wife as I choose my clothes, for qualities that wear well.'

Tracy and I had a hectic social life at this time. Many of the functions she didn't want to attend, but I insisted because I wanted her to meet people from all levels of society. I remember her expression of awe when we walked into the House of Commons on our way to dinner with Margaret Thatcher, who was charm incarnate when we met her.... The night was splashed with a burning sunset over the Thames as we sipped champagne and nibbled caviare and canapés.... I couldn't help thinking, and not for the first time, 'You've not done so bad for a slum kid!'

It's times like that when I wish my parents were still alive. I'm sure that, with a few reservations, they would have been proud of their little son.... I like to think so.

I took Tracy to all my favourite haunts in London, and enjoyed the old city more by seeing it through her eyes. The only cloud on her horizon was that we were not spending enough time at home, and she loved home life passionately. However, there was work to be done. Apart from televising *Blankety Blank*, I was booked for that year's Royal Variety Show, which would be my seventh appearance before Her Majesty ... still a nerve-racking occasion, and all for charity – not even expenses for putting your career on the line.

For sheer panic and bedlam there is nothing to compare with appearing on a Royal Variety show.

The producer has to weld a show together from visiting egotistical Hollywood celebrities, fussy nervous European 'speciality' acts, and ashen-faced comedians and singers. There is never enough dressing-room space so you are crowded into anything that is available and you wait like a modern-day gladiator to do battle for the Emperor's approval. In that interim period twixt rehearsal and performing, you make small talk, you smoke a lot, drink a lot (at least I always did), go over your script again until it begins to sound about as funny as a back issue of the *Radio Times*. At the rehearsal you stand alone on the stage with men banging hammers and doing things with scenery behind you, in the stalls a bored producer listens to your patter without a flicker of emotion, and you desperately want a pee. At the last minute you find a stain on your dress suit and the collar of your shirt has a smudge. Your voice is going and in its place is a raspy drawl and your nerves are as taut as banjo wires.

The Royal Variety Show of 1987 was a variety show in every sense of the word ... Rosemary Clooney, Dolores Grey, James Galway, Johnny Ray, George Shearing and Mel Tormé, Shirley Bassey, Harry Secombe, the new alternative comedians, Hale and Pace, and others too numerous to mention. The show was a hit, and after my spot the Roly Polys joined me in a mock Tiller Girls routine that broke the Royal party up.

Tracy looked divine in a beautiful evening gown and she was the object of a lot of attention at the party afterwards in a famous Mayfair show business hangout. It was an evening of enchantment nearly spoilt by street photographers chasing us as we sped away in a taxi. The difference now was that we could laugh at the silliness of it all.

Pantomime that year was to be in Southampton at the Mayflower Theatre. Once again it was to be *Babes in the Wood* with John Nettles as Sheriff and as principal boy the ex-Miss World beauty queen, Ann Sydney, instead of Ruth Madoc who was appearing in the West End. Allan Stewart, the likeable young Scots comic, and Aiden J. Harvey were joining us as the robbers. The show was being produced as before by Paul Elliot, and we were all looking forward to it immensely, until Paul telephoned me with the bad news that we hadn't done as well with the box office advance in Southampton as in previous years. Frankly, the advance was so small it wouldn't cover two nights' profits; it looked as if we'd bitten off more than we could chew.

It turned out that there had been no publicity and no handbills distributed in the town. We were such a secret, a taxi driver asked me what I was doing in the town. It didn't look good.

John Nettles and I appeared on the local television station in an effort to drum up some interest. I did countless radio interviews and press calls and grinned a lot at passers-by. Slowly the advance bookings crawled up, but it was far from satisfactory and I was opting for a four-week season to grab what there was and head for the hills.

Opening night was packed – not surprising really. It was an 'invited' night for the civic overlords and their guests but I had insisted that a charity be included. The show went well; I ad-libbed more than usual and the crowd loved it. From that opening night the business shot up – good old word of mouth did the trick among the people of Southampton, and we went on to break all records . . . it was also the happiest pantomime I have ever worked in. Apart from the cast, who were marvellous companions, there was an atmosphere about the theatre that gave us all a nightly shot in the arm.

Tracy and I made arrangements to become engaged during the run, and New Year's Eve was the date we agreed on. A big party was being thrown for the cast and we thought it would be great to announce our news then. Unfortunately the press got to hear of our intentions and three of them gatecrashed the party. They were thrown out, but we instantly postponed the planned announcement.

In my heart I had a desire to do something special on our promise to each other. I decided to hold a secret party for Tracy but in a tightly-knit company of show business performers, keeping a secret is about as easy as finding Martin Bormann for *This Is Your Life*. We were staying a couple of minutes' walk away from the theatre in the Polygon Hotel, better known to a generation of travellers as 'The Dead Parrot'. Over the days that followed, ample amounts of booze were hidden in the kitchens of the hotel; pretty dancers organised the decorations, and one of the boy dancers who was a marvellous cook took care of the food. All was set, and Tracy had no idea of the plot afoot. For my part, I'd bought the engagement ring and paid for it with love and a much depleted bank balance. I'd forgotten how expensive these trinkets had become – so long since I'd been involved in the purchase of one. The night of the party arrived and somehow I had to get the entire cast and crew over to the hotel to await Tracy's entrance. The way I did it was a bit cruel.

I lied to her that I had to wait behind in the dressing-room for a phone call. She, poor lamb, was dressed up ready to be taken out, as I'd said that I was taking her to a restaurant and once there, I'd put the ring on her finger. I knew she wasn't exactly thrilled at this; she never said a word in protest, but her wonderful eyes were moist.

The cast left the theatre; only the stage door-keeper remained. Most of the theatre lights had been turned off, my dressing-room alone was still illuminated.

I got the stage door-keeper to come into the dressing-room and say there was a call for me, and he played his role to perfection. When I came back Tracy was sitting with her hands clasped looking a little forlorn.

'That was the restaurant, darling,' I lied. 'Apparently they've had some trouble in the kitchen and all reservations are cancelled for tonight.' I saw her lips tremble and at that moment I hated myself for what I was doing.

'Tell you what, love,' I chirped, 'we'll go over to the hotel and I'll put on a jacket, then we'll go down to the bar, have a quick drink and perhaps a sandwich or a bag of crisps, and I'll put the ring on your finger, angel, and maybe later on we can do it properly.'

Her enormous eyes spoke volumes, and I knew what she had in mind for me and the proposed bag of crisps – and I don't think it was anatomically possible.

We trudged over to the hotel; no one was in sight. I crossed my fingers. It seemed to take an age for the lift to take us to the penthouse suite ... not a sound could be heard from within and I got Tracy to open the door. As she switched the light on, there stood the whole company, cheering and toasting us both, and Tracy's face was wondrous to behold: like a child's upon seeing a Christmas tree. She shed happy tears, and there and then, I went down on one knee, and placed the ring on her finger.

Regretfully that season's pantomime had reached the end of its run and I think I can safely say that each member of the cast was saddened by its closing. We had worked hard and played hard. I had my Tracy and now we could look forward to marriage and a life together.

The following day, we drove away from Southampton and headed for the north and home.

A new chapter was about to open, and I pondered on what it might hold. One thing was for sure, whatever came to challenge me, at least now I had Tracy in the lists with me, and with that knowledge, I knew that I could face any further tribulations.

Just being together was enough for the pair of us, whether in a car or a theatre or at home ... we were a team, and when I kissed her in bed the night we arrived home, I said: 'I'll always love you, forever and a day.' Romantic? Why not, the world would be a better place for a larger helping of it.

I had another book published, a little light soufflé called *Giving Things Up*, and it was time to peddle the book from radio station to radio station and TV station to TV station.

Macmillan were my publishers and they did a very efficient job of getting us from one venue to another. The only trouble was, the book wasn't in the shops at the start of the publicity drive and therefore it was all a bit of a waste of time and energy. These book tours can be quite tiring; one doesn't mind if it's going to be of value in selling the work, but in this case it didn't help one iota and the sales fizzled out like a damp squib. There was also the beginning of a worrying recession in show business. Club dates were drying up as venue after venue closed down. The rise of the cult 'alternative comedy' meant that character comedy was now being looked upon as old-fashioned; in so-called comedy stores, the use of bad language in patter was the norm, and the odd-looking audiences attracted by this sort of entertainment seemed to love it.

To these performers, the lavatory, sexual organs, tampons, body smells were all acceptable subjects for humour, and I could see bad times ahead for the older comedians. I'd noticed with regret that I no longer packed 'em in when I did the odd cabaret date, and even to myself, I sounded ancient....

'My act is so old, I get fan mail from Aesop.'

'I said to my wife, "I'm looking forward to working again, after all there isn't much of it around for comedians." The wife said, "There you go, worrying about other people again."'

'My act has done for comedy what Julie Andrews did for Deep Throat.'

The answer was clear: I had to bring the act up into the modern day. I mean – *Deep Throat* – a film long forgotten except by a very few. . . .

We needed a holiday before the summer season reared its head, and so at the last minute we booked a fortnight in a villa in Lanzarote. I should have known that the imp who besets every holiday I've ever had would make damn sure that this trip to the Canaries, too, would be fraught.

The aeroplane that took us out was so old it ran on Grecian 2000. I don't know how long the plane had been around but we had to take out flying reptile insurance. The pilot couldn't sleep, he kept on having dreams about Zeppelin raids.

We finally bumped to a halt at Lanzarote where the rain was coming down in buckets. The gentleman who was renting us the villa met us at the airport and looked every inch a villain. He pointed out the car we had hired, and I thought it must have featured quite heavily during the week of Comic Relief. It was so small I had to take the windscreen wipers off to get in it. I don't know how old the car was but it didn't have a heater – just a fireplace and a pair of bellows.

The rain intensified as we crawled behind our man from the villa. We inched out way up a slag heap that passed for a mountain, and eventually shuddered to a halt outside a white-painted building.

Behind the villa stood a volcano and the whole area was thick with black volcanic ash, now delightfully waterlogged. It was still bucketing down, and it continued to do so all night as we enjoyed a blazing row as to who was to blame for booking this holiday, the whole purpose of which was to sleep in the sun, swim, and eat health-giving foods.

Now we both realised that it was going to be a battle for survival against a hostile nature. I became morose and started drinking heavily to take my mind off the intense cold and the driving rain. Tracy became morose and started drinking heavily to take her mind off the intense cold and the driving rain.

On the Wednesday, the rain stopped to allow a wind of typhoon proportions to stun us into submission, and Tracy threw her engagement ring at me. It was clear that we were cracking up. I bought more bottles of harsh bootleg alcohol to help us to sleep during one of the periodic hurricanes. By this time Tracy was babbling with hysteria and I, ill shaven and suffering from weight loss, was crying for my mother.

When Saturday arrived, I decided to curtail our vacation. I took this decision after removing a carving knife from Tracy's hand when she attacked me.

I was feeling stronger after my bout of dysentery and eating solids once more, so I asked Tracy to take the bottle of raw spirit out of her mouth and run me into Puerto del Carmen in order to beg the travel agent for a flight home. It was still raining buckets upon the hapless resort.

The nice travel agent said she'd do her best to get us on a flight on Monday, and Tracy tottered into a shop whilst I telephoned home to share my grief with the kids.

Julie answered, and she was tearful. 'Oh Dad,' she

whimpered, 'I've crashed the car and I think I've got whiplash.'

I gripped the receiver, trying to ignore the rain dripping off my nose and the love-smitten poodle that was doing something rude with my right leg. 'Are you all right, sweetheart?' I managed to croak.

'Yes. . . . Here's Pamela.'

Now, Pamela is a drama queen of the highest ham. 'How is Julie?' I asked her, as I nearly kicked the poodle in the jaw.

'HOW SHE WALKED AWAY FROM THE CRASH I'LL NEVER KNOW,' Pamela thundered.

My bowels nearly gave way; I had to get home to my stricken daughter.

We drove the crumbling hire-car back up the slag heap, tumbled into the villa and drank deeply to escape from reality. Tracy had broken out in a rather peculiar rash and I feared that I had contracted cholera and a bit of beri beri.

Time became confused because it was pitch black at noon as the volcanic ash swirled around in the cyclonic winds . . . and yes, it was still bucketing down with rain.

We tried to force a slice of Spanish bread through our blistered lips, and Tracy fried some eggs then had a seizure and threw the pan at a wall.

We clung together under a damp blanket and eventually dropped off to sleep, which was just as well because the need for protein was making me imagine that Tracy was a chicken and I had to battle the temptation to shove her in the oven with some Bisto granules.

However, as I surfaced on Sunday morning, I felt an alien sensation . . . warmth. I rose, trying to call Tracy from unconsciousness, but words wouldn't come from my cracked lips.

'Oh thank you, God,' I croaked and the tears fell as I grovelled on the floor. 'Thank you for letting us live through this holiday.' God had heard our prayers and the sun was shining down on our sodden villa. We pranced out into the garden like pagan children, naked and emaciated, but alive.

At that moment a car bounced to a halt outside the villa, and out climbed the pleasant travel agent with a telegram. I told her that we were now going to stay on for the other week, we shook hands, and the car bounced away. As Tracy and I lounged on deckchairs, getting rapidly braised, she said, 'What was in the telegram, darling?' I passed it over to her.

'Oh dear.... Something's wrong back home,' she cried and handed me back the telegram. I read it and my heart stopped. 'PHONE HOME IMMEDIATELY ... STOP ... VERY URGENT ... YOUR CLEANING LADY,' it said.

I panicked as is my wont and immediately assumed that Julie had either been rushed into hospital after the car crash and was now on the critical list, or that she'd died as a result of her injuries. Tracy caught me as I fell off the deckchair.

We tried all night to get through to England but we couldn't contact anybody at the house, and when I attempted to ring up friends, the line sort of spluttered and once I got faint response from Gibraltar.

Sleep was out of the question and I spent the night pacing to and fro as Tracy lay slumped in a chair, jerking fitfully in a troubled doze. At eight thirty she drove me down the slag heap into Puerto del Carmen and the heat was blistering, but my blood was as cold as chipped ice.

I banged on the door of the travel agency, which seemed to possess the only telephone that worked. Reluctantly a Spanish cleaner let me in.

'Esta muey importante,' I shouted down her ear in my awful Spanish. 'Yo tengo telefono England ... comprende?'

She came close to me and said, 'There's no need to shout, Mr Dawson, I'm not deaf and I'm not Spanish, I'm Miss —— from Ilford.'

I laughed lamely. 'Sorry, you look very sort of ... Spanish ... I must phone my home.'

I dialled our number; my hands were clammy with foreboding.

The cleaning lady who had sent the telegram answered the call. I held myself in readiness for whatever bad news she was about to impart. For Tracy's sake, I had to be strong in the face of whatever tragedy had befallen.... Here is a perfectly true account of the ensuing conversation:

ME: 'Hello, it's Les here.... Yes, Les Dawson.... Yes, yes, the weather's fine.... Yes, yes, Tracy's fine, we're both bloody fine.... Now, what's the matter at home?'

CLEANING LADY: 'You know that carpet you ordered for the hall and stairs? Well, the fellow who's fitting it wants to know are you going to pay before he fits it or after?'

Had the admirable cleaning lady been at my side at that precise moment, I would cheerfully have hacked her to death with a blunt machete. I'd been on the rim of a nervous breakdown, fearing the worst, and she'd sent a telegram over a sodding carpet.

Julie was all right, and oh, Pamela wanted a word with me.

What my daughter had to say made me seethe.... Apparently a newspaper reporter had called at the house and told her that he had heard that I was in Lanzarote with a woman who wasn't Tracy! So they were at it again, hey? We decided to barricade ourselves in the villa in case the press decided to come to the island and look for us.

We resumed our deep sun bathing, both in our birthday suits, and for two days the sun cooked us and only the plaintive mew of a seagull disturbed the silence, and then a small light aircraft came circling over ... getting lower and lower. Once again I jumped to a hasty conclusion – it was the press! We'd show 'em.... We'd give 'em something to photograph. For the next fifteen minutes Tracy and I went through a series of obscenities with our naked bodies that would have delighted the Marquis de Sade.

The plane came down lower and Tracy and I mooned our bare rumps as a sort of grand finale. The wings of the aircraft wobbled, and the thing nearly collided with our volcano. 'That'll teach 'em,' I chortled and we hugged each other like naughty children. Then we sobered up, looked at each other, and with enthusiasm proceeded to do what comes naturally as a sort of encore ... if you see what I mean.

As a postscript to this story, we heard from a resident Britisher on the island that a light aircraft on a training flight had been forced to abort its mission after the young pilots lost concentration whilst watching two naked people engaged in an orgy. The authorities had been informed and word had it that the police suspected a witches' coven.

The last incident to affect this 'holiday' involved a Spanish farmer who had been spying on our nudity for three days from behind a scree mound on the slag heap.

Although the brochure on the villa extolled its utter privacy, it forgot to mention that not all the walls around the place were over six feet in height: the one which ran at the side of the swimming pool at the far end of the property was only two feet high.

The only thing that gave our Peeping Tom away was the sun glinting on his telescope.

I gave vent to a bellow of rage and ran towards him in my bare state shouting 'Bastardo!' He ran like a mountain goat up the black heap and I fell into the swimming pool.

It was with mixed feelings that we left Lanzarote. The weather we were leaving behind was now absolutely glorious and we could have done with another week of it; on the other hand, what we had endured in the name of tourism would probably take years to fade from our minds. But Lanzarote hadn't quite finished with me: my luggage disappeared. I like to sit some nights sipping a Mint Julep and imagining that I have just planted an atomic bomb on Lanzarote, and they have just twenty-four hours to find my suitcase – if not ... no, with my luck the rain would defuse the damn thing.

Once home, we embarked on a hectic schedule. There was a television commercial for toothpaste, some long-haul cabaret dates, and once again, I had another book on the go. I also had to find time to write a couple of newspaper articles as well as be a guest television critic. Finally, there was a frightening income tax problem facing me. At the same time Tracy and I started to talk in earnest about a date for our wedding – a most pleasing task.

I was still contracted to the BBC but I had an uneasy feeling that such was the change taking place in light entertainment generally that it wasn't an alliance destined to last. My agents, Norman and Anne, also saw the signs, and so I started trying to save money as never before. There was the smell of a slump in the air ... unemployment was rising, some smaller businesses were going under in the financial uneasiness, and people weren't going to the theatre so often.

For the summer, I was to headline at the Opera House in Blackpool, which meant that we could enjoy life at home and enjoy a season without having to pay for digs – we could save a bob or two!

Tracy's two children, Samantha and Richard, two fine kids, got on well with Julie, Stuart and Pamela, and although we didn't see them every day of the week, when we did it was wonderful. They'd come to grips with the prospect of having a stepfather who was a bit of a celebrity and indirectly, I think, that fact helped to alleviate any pain that their parents' divorce may have caused.

I signed for another series of *Blankety Blank* and started drafting out an idea for a novel, a spoof on *Gone With The Wind*. I got the daft idea after meeting the film actress, Jane Seymour, during Prince Edward's *It's A Royal Knockout*, which was staged at Alton Towers. During one of the lulls in activity owing to heavy rain, Jane told me that she was in line for a sequel to *Gone With The Wind*. Somehow this sparked off my imagination and I spent the next hour or so mulling over an idea for a send-up of the romantic classic, set in this country. The Confederate States would consist of Lancashire, Cheshire and Yorkshire plus Cumbria, which would break away from the rest of Britain, invade Watford, and start a civil war.... It was a barmy idea: I mean, who the hell would want to invade Watford?

At any rate, I began work on that book, hoping that this time I might produce a bestseller. Up to then, my books had sold only marginally well, and I'd have to sell a lot more if I was ever to achieve my ambition of being a full-time novelist – not to mention keeping a roof over my head.

After Lanzarote, we were kept busy with local social events, and one of the most pleasing was to see the scanner installed in the hospital. Peter Isaacs and I had put a lot of hours into this project and had finally seen his dream come true.

Some months after the installation of the machine, Tracy and I were in Blackpool for the opening night of a play at the Grand Theatre. We were making our way towards the theatre when a small, untidy-looking man grabbed my hand. 'Excuse me, Les,' he said shyly. It turned out he had been under the scanner and whatever it was that had been detected, it had been found in time, and he was now fit and well.

The cabaret work was rapidly drying up; it was things like conferences in London that kept the money rolling in, and I badly needed it because the Inland Revenue were demanding far more than a pound of flesh.

Being in love again was marvellous for me.... I felt ten years younger, and having someone to look after once more was a source of deep happiness. I knew by the look in Tracy's eyes that she was just as happy and contented as I was. We went everywhere together. The long nights in bars with hangers-on and drifters were now over, although to be honest my drinking hadn't abated that much.... I was merely enjoying it more! Tracy hated my habit of smoking over fifty cigarettes a day so I tried to cut down and did partially succeed I think, although I don't imagine for one moment that Tracy would agree on that.

Everything was going great, and the icing on the cake was that I was to top the bill at the Opera House in dear old Blackpool for the summer season. My cup runneth over ... only to be kicked out of my hand by fate.

When the Laughter had to Stop

The audience would soon see the little fat man wheeze on to the enormous stage and after pulling some silly faces he would launch into a string of hospital and medical jokes....

'My doctor is very old-fashioned. He'll retire soon, he's running out of leeches.'

'He doesn't believe in pain killers ... he makes you bite on a bullet. If you haven't any teeth, he'll rent you a pair – his brother is an undertaker.'

'I was in hospital recently ... hospital, that's a place where they wake you up to give you a sleeping pill.'

'One nurse gave me so many enemas, they had to weld an extension on the bedpan.'

What the audience didn't see was the scene in the dressing-room before the little comedian went on stage: his wife watching him cough his heart up over the sink; the anxiety in her eyes as he tried to rub some colour into his grey face. He tried to make a joke about his condition, but he didn't make her smile.

The Opera House, Blackpool, is possibly one of the largest theatres in Europe. It seats over three thousand people – that's a lot of backsides, brother.

Over the years, the old place has seen some of the greatest variety shows ever staged. George and Alfred Black used to take the andience's breath away with lines of gorgeous dancers, wonderful costumes and extravagant sets. However, of late, owing to cash flow problems and increased costs, much smaller productions had been staged and they hadn't done so well. Like Max Bygraves and Ken Dodd, I had done many Sunday night concerts there and had always packed them in, and so I looked forward with eagerness to appearing there for eighteen weeks.

My agents assured me that they had been assured that the company putting on the show would spare no expense, and that we'd give the ghosts of George and Alfred Black something to haunt about. I was content to let them take care of things whilst I finished my television commitments.

I arrived at the Opera House for the first day's rehearsal and sat next to my producer and friend from television, Stewart Morris. Together we watched six young dancers go through a routine. I turned to Stewart and whispered, 'Isn't the full dance company rehearsing?' He looked at me strangely and replied, 'What on earth are you talking about? That's it, six dancers, that's the company.'

I froze. The Opera House stage is so vast you could service two Boeing 747s on the apron of it and still have room to build some bungalows – and a day-care centre as well. Six dancers would be lost in that gigantic area.

The bill consisted of, apart from myself, the Roly Polys, Frank Carson, Keith Harris and two unknown performers who had only just started in the business. Jerry Allison, the bandleader, a nice guy who was to die tragically soon afterwards, worked with me in an effort to instill some life into the production. We did our best. I had managed to get two more dancers, but that was it . . . and here we were on opening night. Jerry and the boys struck up the overture, I walked on to the stage and pretended to be the bandleader as the curtain went up. It is a strange anomaly in show business that rehearsals always seem to be dispirited, and yet once the curtain goes up on opening night a magic seems to fill the theatre and every artiste appears to take on a newer, fresher persona.

'Good evening. May I say what a thrill it is to be in Blackpool – which as you know is Morecambe with "O" levels.'

'It's so healthy here – that fresh air – a mixture of ozone and chip fat.'

'They say the sea here at Blackpool is polluted – rubbish . . . mind you, there's not many places where you see fish swimming with surgical boots on.'

'I live in St Annes – so posh – when we eat cod and chips there we wear a yachting cap.'

The opening gags went well enough, but I was conscious that there were empty seats . . . and believe me, dear reader, there were a considerable number of them. The Roly Polys were a sensation; I'm always proud of them. Frank Carson brought the house down with his Irish blarney, and Keith Harris with Orville the Duck and his other inventive puppets had the audience in stitches. The other two less experienced performers had a struggle to overcome their nerves as well as their awe of working in such an august theatre. Nevertheless, despite the valiant efforts of all the performers, I knew by the reaction of the crowd at the opening night party that we'd laid an egg. The critics cut the show to pieces, and me they shredded.

I began to have misgivings about my ability to top a

bill any more; I ignored Tracy's protests and took my self-pity to a bottle of Scotch. I think I caused her a lot of worry during that season; little did she know that without her support I would probably have walked out....

Whom had I let down? Instead of acting like a pro and making the best of it, I brooded over the lack of interest from the public and my own performance – which had come in for a lot of comment, 'old-fashioned' being about the kindest.

I was hurt, and I felt stress taking over my every sinew. Walking on to the stage night after night was not a task I looked forward to. One or two reporters were still peeping at us and taking secret photographs, which was irritating to say the least.

One Sunday morning my son nearly killed himself in my 'E' type Jaguar. God only knows how he escaped from the tangled mess of metal.... As he lay in the hospital bed I thanked God for a miracle.

I was smoking cigarette after cigarette and I simply couldn't relax. The poor business at the theatre was common knowledge and I felt that every artiste in the town was gossiping about me. I was becoming paranoid.

Sunday morning, and it was a hot one. Tracy and I are sitting by the small swimming pool in our back garden. I sip my drink and try to take my mind off the problems, but it isn't easy and I can't completely, because there is a slight burning sensation in my chest ... just an irritation, but it won't go away.

Friends and family come and go and occasionally Tracy will dive into the pool and call to me to join her. I shake my head. This burning is getting to be a nuisance, and it's making me feel sick.

It is a warm day and I am sweating profusely ... try

another drink, hey? Ah, that's a bit easier, I'll light up a fag, stuff the income tax and sod the show ... grab the money and run.... It's like a hot ball of acid in my chest ... bloody uncomfortable, must go in the kitchen and swallow a couple of Rennies, perhaps that will shift it ... Tracy's asking me if I'm OK, she says I look a bit pale.

Darkness, and still can't sleep with this infernal burning. Might as well get out of bed and let Tracy sleep.... I like to watch her when she sleeps. She has the face of a child and her tumbling hair cascades around her on the pillow.

I walk in the garden. It's creeping on towards dawn – the best time to be out.

I draw deep on a cigarette and try to ignore the acid in my body, but it will not be ignored.... It's burning, burning in my chest.

All day the burning is still there, and we go to the theatre earlier than normal because I'm uncomfortable in the house, I don't feel right, I need space.

The company manager comes into the dressing-room, looks at me and asks if I feel all right.... *Of course I'm all right.... It's this bloody indigestion.* Showtime, open the show, not many people in the theatre.... Christ, it's so hot.... Come off and slump in dressing-room. Tracy is suddenly looking worried and she's firm.... What's that she's doing? No, Tracy, don't send for the theatre doctor.... He's here, but I'm due on stage again in ten minutes.

The doctor, Bob Wells, looks concerned, says I should go to Victoria Hospital for a check-up.... How can I go? What about the show?

Suddenly there's a different Tracy, this one is angry ... what's she saying? To hell with the show? She's making me take off my stage suit and don my jeans and T-shirt.

Frank Carson and the Roly Polys gather round with Keith Harris and they're being pros and altering the programme.... Seems stupid, it's only indigestion.

Sitting on a trundle bed in the hospital, someone is injecting me.... Hey? There's Stuart and Julie and Tracy and Pamela.... Hi, everybody. Can't seem to speak properly.... God, I feel so tired....

I awoke the following morning to learn that I had suffered a heart attack. Tracy was at my bedside where she'd been since I was admitted. Now I felt great and wanted to be up and about, but the young doctor restrained me. 'I know, Les, you don't feel ill, but believe me, although the heart attack was a mild one, it is a warning, my friend.... You've got to slow down.' He said it in such a way, I knew he was right.

Tracy gripped my hands and looked deep into my eyes. 'I love you, Lumpy, but from now on you are going to do as you're told,' she said softly but firmly, and kissed me.

Me, do what I'm told? Me, the old hell-raiser who never went to bed before dawn and drank everyone around me under the table? Matt Monroe, Dave Allen, Tommy Cooper, I'd caroused with the best.... Me, do what I'm told? I didn't argue, I simply nodded to Tracy and muttered, 'Whatever you say, angel,' and dropped into a black lagoon.

I don't think I've ever slept so much and for so long. All the years of push and push, making do with a catnap, all those years of being eaten up with ambition – well, sleep got in the way, it was a waste of life, wasn't it? Now, my worn-out and abused body had stated that enough was enough, buster.

I lay in that hospital bed with wires poking out of my

chest and machines going bleep and I felt depressed and useless. I couldn't believe a heart attack had happened to me – I wasn't old enough, surely – cardiac arrests were something that occurred in old men who wore panama hats ... but here I was. The artistes dutifully trooped to my bedside and Mo, from the Roly Polys, played merry hell with me for overdoing it and worrying; so did Russ Abbot, and Frank Carson, whose voice could warn shipping in the Solent, told me a stream of old Irish jokes at which I laughed loudly, hoping by doing so to get rid of the old ham.

Tracy came, and brought a ray of sunshine with her. How I loved this girl; for her and our future, I resolved to get well and lead a more intelligent life. Life was too precious to allow mundane materialism and the pursuit of ambition to destroy the things that really mattered. Trouble was, I'd said all this before, this time would I take heed?

It may sound silly, but I think it might be a good idea if we all had to spend an occasional day in hospital.... Not only would it make us realise how frail the human condition is, but we would see the selfless devotion shown by those who work in the healing centres.... I have seen a lot of hospitals, God only knows, what with Meg's long illness, and my own brush with death when my prostate gland operation went badly wrong.... I remember also a morning in Southampton when the cast from the pantomime at the Mayflower Theatre visited a children's ward. I signed a photograph for a little girl who had terminal cancer. Her father had spoken to me at length, asking how I coped with the death of Meg. He even asked me whether I believed in God.... He desperately wanted an answer as to why his precious child should have to die.... He looked at me with eyes so sunken with despair that I lied and lied.... Yes, I remember saying, a cure is just around the corner.... Yes, I'd said, of course I believed in God.... Of course one copes with death, after all, the loved one is only slipping out of the room, she is still in the house, I lied.... The man's eyes thanked me for the words, even though he knew as well as I that I was lying.

As expected the newspapers had a field day with my heart problems. One tabloid's headline read rather breathlessly: 'Dawson staggered into the arms of his barmaid lover'. I don't mind a newspaper proffering a juicy story providing it's true; but I draw the line when the story has no foundation in fact.

However, on the credit side, many of the tabloids rang up and wished me a speedy recovery and once again sent flowers. One or two freelance photographers skulked outside the hospital and gleefully snapped Tracy in a large black hat and sunglasses as she left to go home, and in the following morning's papers she looked as if she'd just betrayed Al Capone.

Meanwhile I moved to a private hospital in order to free my bed in Victoria for a more needy case, and frankly the press had been getting on the nerves of the overworked staff. We rather astounded the staff at the very luxurious South Fylde Hospital because Tracy insisted upon staying in the room with me! She got her way despite the opposition, and a small trundle bed was wheeled in. We were together. On one occasion I awoke in the night to find a stern nurse hovering in the doorway, obviously making sure that we were not doing anything naughty. It made us both laugh the first time, then the interruptions became a trifle more frequent and I began to consider charging a fee for admittance.

The Krankies had come in to replace me in the Opera

House, and from all accounts were doing better business . . . and that information didn't cheer me up one iota.

Doctors came and doctors went: they looked at me, then poked and prodded my inert mass and tutted a lot in the process. 'LOSE WEIGHT' was one battle cry, another was 'STOP SMOKING'. I cringed at yet another doom-laden warning: 'DON'T DRINK ALCOHOL IN EXCESS'. Those edicts were merely the skirmishers before the main assault began.

'Mr Dawson,' one bloodless pipe-stem of a female dietician roared at me. 'No sugar, no cakes, no pastry, no beer, no cheese. Less salt, preferably none at all, no white bread, no butter or margarine . . . no spirits!' Jesus! I wanted to shout, why did you keep me alive? 'Don't be so ridiculous, Les,' said one white-coated fiend, 'you can have lots of goodies on a diet: nut fritters, celery, lots and lots of lettuce, fish, boiled or grilled – not fried – and no chips.' What? Fish without chips? Whatever happened to the British Empire? Chicken? Oh, I don't mind that. What? Chicken without the skin? But that's the best part of the bloody fowl!

I grew cunning even with my loved ones. I had to survive the hospital somehow. I paid a backward orderly a king's ransom for a bar of nut chocolate which I hid under my mattress and ate when everybody was asleep.

Tracy bought me fruit, especially bananas. Within a week I was walking around on my knuckles and showing my bum to everybody.

The orderly put the screws on me when I begged him to buy me a Cornish pasty. . . . What I should have done in the face of such overt blackmail was to stab him with a thermometer, but my cravings were too great, and I pushed an extra pound in his hand as an incentive for him to purchase said pie and get it back without detection.

The crumbs I kept in a paper bag in case I felt peckish during the night ... which I always did, of course.

I found a cigarette end in an abandoned ashtray and you might have thought I'd discovered the Koh-i-noor diamond. When Tracy went for a bath, I slipped out of the room and sneaked into a staff toilet. I lit up my cigarette butt and choked and coughed in sheer ecstasy. My hospital room was full of flowers which I ate inside a pillowcase.

Finally – and gladly – the staff sent me home, but not before urging me to use another hospital next time ... if there was a next time, not on your life, I thought, flowers give me wind.

I stood outside the hospital with Tracy and I felt as though I'd been released from San Quentin. No matter how luxurious, a hospital is still a place of incarceration. The sun was shining and the reporters were out there gripping their pencils in readiness for a story, and I hammed it up....

REPORTER: How do you feel, Les, after your heart attack?
ME: I still feel with my right hand, and my heart never attacked anybody.
REPORTER: About the future ... any thoughts of marriage?
ME: Certainly not, I hardly know you.
REPORTER: Come on, you and Tracy, when are you going to tie the knot?
ME: After the baby's been delivered I should think.

Of course the reporter's little ears shot up – was my blonde barmaid ripe with child?

I frankly didn't give a damn what he printed, but he realised eventually that the whole interview was a gag, and strode away irritated.

We posed for a photograph and then drove back to Garth House and food ... real food, and sod the calories.

Tracy looked after me and refused to let me use the phone, and visits from relatives and friends were curtailed. I recuperated, and for three weeks it was a joy to roam around the garden, prod at the odd weed and drink a lot of tea, but then the workaholic took over and I lusted to start work again. However, in Tracy I had found not just a new love, I'd found a woman with a will of iron!

Trying to have the odd smoke was out, because her sense of smell was so acute, she could stand on the landing in Lytham and smell bacon burning in Glasgow. I'd met my match, but the knowledge only served to increase my cunning little ways.... I hid fags all over the place and encouraged Tracy to go shopping. She did – and the shopping expeditions were so expensive I had to sell all the cigarettes I'd hidden in order to avoid bankruptcy. To get round that problem, I invited all my heavy-smoking friends round, and then I would sit downwind and breathe in the wonderful aroma. That only happened once because Tracy told everyone that smoking was taboo if I was to live through the night, and so my so-called friends refused to light up when they came to visit.

Three weeks, and not one cigarette passed from the packet to my lips.... It was not easy. I chewed gum, ate sweets, drew on an empty pipe and sobbed openly. Tracy had noted the doctor's warning that I should cut down on alcohol and, cold-hearted wanton that she was, she made sure that not a drop of the Devil's Brew was in evidence. On top of everything else, I was forbidden to do pantomime at Bristol that Christmas, something I had been looking forward to ever since I'd taken part in a grand press launch there some months before.

For the first time in my life I was frightened.... Everything that I'd taken for granted was no longer there; my health was suspect; and I began to feel that nobody wanted me any more. When the television was on, I'd moodily watch the new wave comedians and that would plunge me into a deeper hole of depression. That Tracy put up with me at that period of time can only be a measure of her love for me.... Thanks, kid.

Through a contact of ours with Cunard, I managed to secure a ten-day cruise on the liner *Canberra*. It was a semi-working trip in the sense that in return for having photographs taken with the captain and crew, we would be given a big price concession on a stateroom....

Tracy packed enough clothes to fill the average C&A store and I, with my vast knowledge of cruising, took one suitcase in contrast to her seven.

The imp of mischief struck the holiday almost immediately ... Tracy's seven pieces of luggage came safely on board the ship, mine didn't. As the liner churned away from Southampton dock, one solitary suitcase stood on the end of the jetty: mine. It finally came on board at Lisbon, so at least I could wear fresh underpants in case I had an accident and fell off the ship. Despite Tracy's protests, I started smoking again and with the swell of the sea, the bar was the only place to be in, wasn't it? Working on the premise that if you can't beat 'em, then join 'em, Tracy propped the bar up with me.

The weather was the worst in living memory. The sun fitfully poked its head through the black clouds for about half an hour a day, and we all discarded our vomit buckets and rushed up on deck to marvel at the unaccustomed warmth.

The weather was so bad the captain couldn't dock the ship at Gibraltar. Once again, I was experiencing a true Dawson holiday. At the end of it Tracy and I came ashore feeling ready for a holiday, and lounged about the house for the next two weeks.

Meanwhile the income tax demand wouldn't go away, and I was still mourning the fact that my watch, bracelet and diamond ring had been stolen from my cabin as I lay on my bunk in a drunken torpor.... Oh, didn't I mention the theft? I had foolishly gone down into the crew's quarters and we had drunk the night away, and I had got robbed for my pains....

It is my fervent belief that God needs something to laugh at, and I'm it. Years ago, I took out an insurance book. My mother lent me the money to buy the book and lo! I was a fully fledged insurance representative. Nobody had prepared me for such an occupation: my area was a tough, rough, working-class part of Manchester and they only bought small policies – enough to bury a relative and a bit over for a vase.

I'd spend half an hour crouched over a premium book writing down '2p on Alfred ... 4p on John'. Half an hour – and then I'd emerge from the two-up and two-down with sixpence in my bag. I couldn't sell new insurance to anybody, and there were murmurs for my dismissal.

I'd bought myself a second-hand bicycle and a new air pump because the tyres were so bald they looked as if they'd been backcombed. For some obscure reason, some idiot was going around stealing bicycle pumps, so I used to take mine off the bike and carry it round with me.... That was fine until one gloomy day I entered a terraced house brandishing my briefcase and my pump. The old lady I'd gone to see didn't enjoy the best of eyesight and screamed when she saw the pump, thinking it was some sort of cosh. Her son rushed into the room and grabbed my arms, and it was a rather ugly scene until they realised who I was and what I was carrying. To make amends, the old lady made me a cup of tea and handed me a bloater paste sandwich. When I said goodbye to her, I walked into the street and found that someone had stolen my bike.

I was so angry I marched into the local police station, waving my pump, and informed them of the theft of my bicycle. One florid copper with a warped sense of humour remarked, when I asked him how I was going to get home, 'Shove the pump between your legs and use it as a jet.'

Some work came my way: heaven-sent commercials for paint and cakes. These small engagements helped to stave off famine and keep my hand in. Christmas came and went, and in the early new year of 1989, Tracy and I made our date with matrimony. It was to be on her birthday, 6 May.

bove) One of the happiest oments in Meg's life – the night ne met Cary Grant. Amazing ally, we could have been taken r twins, old Cary and I *(Yorkshire Evening Post)*.

very brave little lady indeed – eg and I at the Water Rats' Ball. was to be her last public appearance. I didn't know then how soon I would lose her *(Paul Smith)*.

Eric Sykes and I at Blackpool where we appeared in *Run For Your Wife* together. We ad libbed so much that the play overran every night. At one performance, there was a Just Married couple in the front row – when the play finally ended, they had three kids. (*Evening Gazette, Blackpool*)

Princess Michael of Kent and Yours Truly backstage at the Palace Theatre, Manchester, during the run of *Babes in the Wood* – I'm the shorter one (*Manchester Daily Mail*).

In my rôle as Nurse Ada, note the necessary props. Some people firmly believed that my interpretation of a woman was enough to cure the average peeping Tom.

Myself delivering an ultimatum from the *Tailor and Cutter* to John Nettles. His hair was cut during a plague scare. Some kind cynic reported that when John and I appeared together only one thing spoilt our performances – the seats faced the stage *(E & B Promotions)*.

6 May 1989. Tracy becomes my wife in a moving and warm ceremony that held laughter and joy in the ritual. My son, Stuart, and stepson, Richard, look on approvingly as the clergyman, Mr Baker, scores with yet another great gag – my agent offered him six weeks on the pier at Cromer.

Well, that's that, my turtle dove. Now, about the honeymoon night . . . even thinking about it has brought colour to my cheeks.

(above left) My bride and I enjoying our honeymoon in dear old Scotland. We had a week out of time, a castle, a piper, the splash of salmon and the crash of stags in the forest deep. We did a lot of other things, but that's our business! *(above right)* Man's best friend is a St Bernard pup ... until it reaches the size of our Delilah. Thumper and Patch, the rabbits, have just tabled a motion, can you blame 'em?

Time off for pleasure in the Isle of Man with Chris de Burgh and Norman Wisdom at the opening of Kevin Woodward's restaurant. I did once have a photo taken without a drink in my hand!

The 1991 Royal Variety Show from the old Victoria Palace. Although I scored a personal triumph, Her Majesty didn't mention adoption *(Doug McKenzie)*.

Just an informal chat you understand.... I'm not quite sure who the other chap is.... *(Doug McKenzie)*.

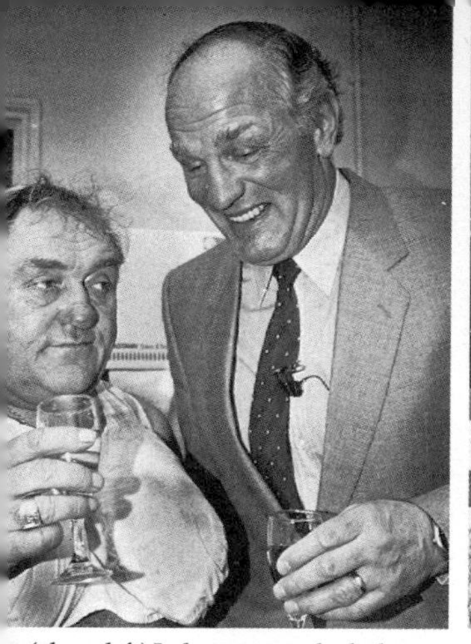

(above left) I always concluded every pantomime by saying: 'You've been a great audience and would you please put your hands together for a visiting celebrity ... the one and only ... Henry Cooper.' Oh, sorry, missis! Without my knowing, Henry had crept into the theatre in Southampton for our final performance of the panto and blew the gag! It's a good job for him that I'd lost my shorts and gum shield.

(above right) Switching on the Blackpool illuminations. What an honour – I would have done it for nothing. Wait a minute, I did!

The cast of the play *Run For Your Wife*. We posed for this during an extensive tour – we'd been on the road so long that we all suffered from a tarmac rash.

Tracy and I after we had just been told the great news that we were expecting a baby. And I thought Tracy was suffering from excess wind. Our joy knew no bounds....

For Better or for Worse!

The guests watched the little bridegroom adjust the microphone in readiness for a toast to the bridesmaids. They saw him remove the large cigar from his lips and start cracking gags about the state of marriage....

'Marriage is an institution, and that's where a couple usually finish up.'

'Compromise is the secret of a happy marriage. My next-door neighbour wanted a second-hand car, his wife wanted a fur coat. They couldn't afford both, so they compromised ... she got the coat but they keep it in the garage.'

'Tracy and I have had a slight disagreement. I've gone to a hell of a lot of trouble to book a caravan for her honeymoon.... Would you believe she doesn't want to go in a caravan? She wants to come to the South of France with me.'

What the guests couldn't see was a heart overflowing with love and gratitude to God for allowing me so much happiness.

Tracy wanted a quiet wedding.... I didn't.

Tracy fancied going abroad somewhere and getting married on the beach. I didn't like that idea one bit because with my track record, the chances were we'd end up clinging to a broken mast in the Indian Ocean after a cyclone.

No, I was insistent, we had to stage a big wedding so that all would see our union. Somebody leaked the news of our impending nuptials to the press and they started badgering us again, this time for an exclusive coverage of the event.... Instead I decided to invite all the major newspapers to the ceremony.

Like every wedding, it was a time of chaos; who should be invited and who should not.... How many bridesmaids, what about flowers, drink, the venue for the reception – the way the list of guests was growing we'd probably need Wembley Stadium.

Tracy's friend Christine was to make her wedding dress, which was going to be white to symbolise the purity of our union. For me, a visit to Moss Bros for the traditional top hat and tails – that I agreed to wear this sort of outfit must surely be a measure of my love for Tracy, because quite frankly, with my figure I look like a beached sperm whale in it.

Stuart, my son, was to be my best man, and Pamela and Julie two of the bridesmaids. I blanched at the sheer cost of the forthcoming venture!... Tracy still argued that we should slip away to an island in the sun and get married on a beach.... No, no, I snarled, we're going to show all the gossips that our love was made in heaven. Before the actual ceremony I talked to Meg's headstone, and I know she approved the undertaking.

There was one slight hitch. My Golf Classic that we held in May for charity, fell on 8 May, which meant that we would have to delay our honeymoon. We still hadn't decided where to go for it, and at this stage there was only a fortnight left.

Two things transpired which proved to me that Fate was being kind. My agents, Norman and Anne, rang up to inquire, with tongue in cheek, just how much I reckoned the wedding was going to cost. I trembled. My pencil dangled from my lifeless fingers. The wedding list had grown to lavish proportions and I had put down a figure of over twenty thousand pounds as an estimate. Norman knew that my tax bill had neatly cleared out a substantial sum, and casually said, 'I think we can help. We've got a Ford commercial on television for you to do ... that should pay for the wedding and a bit left over.'

I could have kissed him ... well, almost.

Peter Harrison, an old friend, directed the commercial and we had two wonderful days shooting it and enjoying Peter's hospitality. He and I had worked once before on a TV ad for cream cakes and after the shoot had been wrapped Tracy and I and all the crew drank a bathful of champagne and piled on the calories with fresh cream cakes ... sheer heaven.

The next thing that occurred was that friends of ours in the Isle of Man, Stuart Jameson and his lovely wife Geraldine, told us that as a wedding gift they were going to arrange and pay for our honeymoon.

The hectic countdown began in earnest. Dresses for the bridesmaids, outfits for the best man and the ushers ... the cost was creeping up. The champagne had been ordered, but good grief, would the guests really get through that vast amount? The wedding cake, oh yes, three tiers – I was going to be in tears if the cost didn't stop mounting. I had nightmares about strong men frog-marching me to court with a host of creditors demanding the return of capital punishment. The cars, all vintage, had been ordered, and the cost leapt up and was given a further boost by the bill for the flowers.... There were to be flowers everywhere, on the altar, under the altar, up the vicar's surplice and in my lady's chamber.

I was totally ignored as I dashed to and fro waving bills in the air. Everybody was too busy with the wedding to spare a thought for me – after all, I was merely the bridegroom....

Gleefully, I counted on a lot of the guests not being able to make the wedding. I argued that would help save a copper or two ... but no, all the replies came back saying 'Yes, we'd love to come.'

The rehearsals for the wedding came and went, people pulled me into different positions and all the attention was naturally focused on the bride to be. I was simply there as ballast.

The last days sped by and we grew nervous and snapped at each other.... I thought of all the wedding jokes I'd cracked:

'Marriage, the only union without a shop steward.'

'The bride was so fat I put the ring on her finger with a tyre lever.'

'The vicar said, 'Do you take this woman or is it Candid Camera?'

'My bride was so fat, when I carried her over the threshold I made three trips.'

The night before the wedding, I was thrown out of my own home by a band of zealous women. I barely had time to shout goodbye to Tracy before being bundled off the premises.

My stag night was a positive cornucopia of booze. I stayed the night at a friend's house and we drank and talked about the old days, drank some more and then talked about the old days, then Richard, my pal, shoved me in the general direction of bed. Sleep was impossible.

Not only did the bedroom keep whirling round, I kept wondering if I was doing the right thing....I was marrying a woman a lot younger than myself, my kids were grown up, and here I was about to become a stepfather to Richard and Samantha, both still youngsters not even on the verge of their teens.... What about my health? Would I be able to stand up to it all?

Finally, as dawn poked its fingers through the bedroom window, I sank into a deep sleep.

The house was full of noise, and my head played a pretty low key descant to the household cacophony. Richard's wife gave me breakfast and cauldrons of coffee; I was pushed under a shower, taken out and given a large Scotch.... Ah! thank God for true friends.

The morning fled by, and to add to my nervous twitches, word arrived that already there was a huge crowd outside the White Church on Clifton Drive.... How the hell did they know this was the day? I hadn't blabbed it, had I?

More Scotch, and there's my son, Stuart, looking very handsome in his grey tails, he tells me that there's a swinging party going on back home at Garth House.... According to him, the house is awash with people eating and drinking.... I begin to wish we'd sailed to a remote atoll near Samoa and done the deed there with some beach bum as a witness.

Richard, Derek, Stuart, my son, and Stuart, my friend, made four superbly garbed ushers. Together with John, the elegantly dressed young man who was to become my son-in-law, they gazed at me owlishly as the final minutes on the clock ticked away my bachelorhood. Another glass of the spirit and another cigarette ... *it is the time.* My top hat fell off twice as I wriggled into the car and my shirt button, the first one you'd notice, flew off.

There was silence in the car as we drove to the church, and when we saw the milling hordes outside, the only word to break the silence came from me ... 'Shit.'

The crowds roared as I got out of the car, the photographers kneeling in ranks blasted off roll after roll of film, and the flashlights blinded me. I stumbled over my trouser bottoms, which had descended to an all-time low thanks to a pair of faulty braces. This naturally got an enormous laugh and I jammed the top hat over my eyes for an encore.

The inside of the church was akin to the Black Hole of Calcutta.... I have never seen so many people in so small a space before, and from every pew hung giant garlands of flowers. The scent of the blooms – not to mention the armies of greenfly crawling up my sleeve – made me dizzy. I sat there alongside my son and waited ... and waited ... and waited: no bride in sight. 'That's it,' I thought, 'she's not coming, she's buggered off, there will be no wedding....' How could I escape from the church and avoid the press? I could see the headlines in the tabloids ... 'Dawson dumped'. My son tried to reassure me, he tried to make me laugh, but all I could muster was a sickly grin. Then suddenly the crowd stirred, the music 'Somewhere in Time' struck up; Tracy, my bride, had finally made it.

The congregation stood as she made her way down the aisle on the arm of Len, our dear friend who was giving her away, and when I saw her my throat constricted ... she looked absolutely beautiful. Her natural radiance shone through and was complemented by her wedding dress. I couldn't stop the tears from springing to my eyes, and I wished for her sake that her mother and father could have been alive to see her.

All the bridesmaids were a picture to behold.... Marion, Tracy's lovely sister; Tracy's friend, Wendy, daughters Julie and Pamela, and Tracy's daughter, Samantha, looking so much more mature than her ten summers. Richard, Tracy's son, even managed to forget football for the time being as he revelled in his role as pageboy.

The vicar, Mr Baker, started off the ceremony by wishing Tracy a happy birthday, and dammit if he didn't crack a few gags – and got big laughs! Frankly, I have never been fond of church services, there always seems to be an air of pious misery about them, as if to be happy has no place in worship.... But this wedding ceremony was so full of laughter that the church became a warm and wonderful place, and I thought how many more folk would be attracted to services if laughter and a more light-hearted approach were to be encouraged.... And as the shafts of sunlight lasered through the stained glass windows, highlighting the mellow antiquity of the pews and shimmering around the beautiful bride who had deigned to be my wife, I distinctly smelt the scent of freesias.

A close friend, Jackie Scott, sang the haunting song 'Wind Beneath My Wings', and when Tracy and I came out of the vestry, now Mr and Mrs Dawson, everyone in the whole church rose and clapped and beamed at two people who had found each other and joined souls.

Was there ever such a day! The weather was glorious. Outside the church the vast crowds surged forward and the smiling but perspiring policemen tried valiantly to hold them back in a good-natured fashion. They had to give it up, and our car was besieged by well-wishers as we sipped champagne in the veteran Rolls Royce, supplied as a wedding present by Peter Hall, a friend from Essex.

Show business pals kept the crowds happy, and Tracy and I drove in a cloud of bliss to the Imperial Hotel for the reception. The press followed, they were enjoying the day as much as everyone else. Of course Fate had to put a slight dampener on a Dawson event.... Because of security at the Imperial Hotel during the recent Tory conference, all the windows in the huge dining-room had been screwed down and could not be opened, and the heat was now more intense than ever.

Five hundred guests, the Northern Dance Orchestra, a full disco set-up and a trio playing on the balcony, plus a horde of scurrying waiters, served to heat the place to the temperature of a furnace, and there was a grave possibility of dehydration. That, fortunately, was prevented by a mass guzzle of champagne. I thanked the Lord that my bank manager was on holiday.

Tracy and I were at last man and wife, and all the past sadness in our lives had vanished into the shadows of yesterday. What had seemed a barren future after Meg had passed away was now a fertile promise for me; Tracy had brought sunshine into my life and lifted the weight of depression off my shoulders. We held each other close on the dance floor, oblivious of everyone around us....

Two days after the wedding I officiated at my Golf Classic, and the following day we boarded a chartered aircraft at Blackpool Airport, bound for Inverness. As I have mentioned our honeymoon had been arranged for us as a wedding present by the Jamesons, but they had kept the details a secret. A car would meet us at Inverness and take us to our destination – we knew no more than that.

The flight was smooth and the charter company threw in a couple of bottles of champagne for good measure, and we set foot in Scotland in a somewhat advanced state of alcohol addiction.

Sure enough, a car was waiting for us, its driver a very agreeable Scotsman in a bright kilt who looked like a print of Rob Roy. It was a marvellous, long, winding journey through rolling hills with steely mountains in the background. Deer and other wild life bounded. Once or twice we stopped and alighted to admire the stunning scenery, and there and then I fell in love with the Highlands.

Although no stranger to Scotland, I had previously only played the clubs in Glasgow and Edinburgh, and some of those had been so tough that if the audience liked you they didn't clap, they let you live. I remember appearing in one exquisite dump with a bouncer on the door who threw drunks *in*! The Glasgow Empire ... the name still sends a chill up the seasoned performer's spine. I'm not saying that I died there, but an undertaker in the audience threw a tape measure at me and some embalming fluid.

I still shudder at the recollection of telling a joke about a Scotsman who was so mean, when he found his wife with another man he made them stand one behind the other so that when he shot them both it would only take one bullet.... I nearly had to take a tar and feather insurance out for that one!

But these Highlands: they were a side of Scotland I'd never seen before and I looked forward to reaching our destination.

Our car finally bumped across a moat and stopped outside a small castle on a thickly forested island. We had arrived. Standing on a high cairn of stones was a piper playing us in with a traditional welcome. Lined up at the front entrance were the staff who were to look after us – it was like a scene from a historical film, as each lady curtsied to us and bade us both welcome to the castle.

Drinks were waiting for us in the high vaulted reception room where the walls were adorned with plaids, and fine prints hung above a wide stone fireplace. The floor was flagged and the staircase wound dreamily upwards to panelled corridors where portraits of fierce, proud men stared from the walls. There was a timeless quality about the castle and one fully expected to hear the swish of crinoline skirts gliding along the passages. It was quite enchanting.

Tracy and I were shown to our bedroom, which was just slightly bigger than the Isle of Man. We gazed at the massive bed, then at each other; then, when the twinkling-eyed lady who'd escorted us to the bedroom curtsied and left us alone, we gazed at the bed again and did what comes naturally for a very entertaining hour or so.

Betsy, the cook, was a fine big lady whose meals were worthy of an international gourmet's consideration. Fresh salmon, pheasant, mouth-watering soups and steaks.... Oh dear, the weight was already piling on.... It was a week out of time for both of us, and what made it all the more enchanting was that when our little staff had gone home for the evening, Tracy and I had the castle to ourselves ... we were the only guests there.

We made a habit of dressing up for dinner, and Tracy would sit at one end of the long, elegant dining table and I at the other. Betsy had sternly instructed us to use the bell under the table to summon the food and wine.... Ah! the wine.... Dark rich burgundies and naughty-looking clarets.... I was burping vintage wind by now.

Sleep was never far away: the air was so rarefied and clean, when it swept into our bedroom it massaged us in a gentle rippling motion that sent us tumbling into a deep, peaceful abyss....

In the morning, Betsy would rouse us with two huge mugs of hot tea, then she would march back in with a breakfast of eggs, bacon, ham, sausage, cereals, toast, marmalade, orange juice and fried potato hash.... By the time we'd devoured that, we needed a rope ladder to climb up over our stomachs.

Tracy would make me walk for miles along the banks of a mirror-surfaced loch, and we'd sit and drink in the beauty of this exquisite paradise of soaring peaks and silent, plunging valleys; gnarled trees that seemed older than time itself crouched over in escort duty on either side of the meandering paths that took two lovers on a breathless tour.... The only sounds that broke through the screen of lichen-encrusted trees were the crash of a stag through the undergrowth or the splash of a salmon trout in the river.

Never have I known such a happy time: restored to health, in love, married to a wonderful girl – all the urgent search for ambition and power now seemed so mundane compared to my present state of tranquillity. It was impossible not to believe in a Higher Being.

All too swiftly the honeymoon came to an end, and now our piper on the high cairn of stones played a lament, and dear Betsy and her ladies lined up to bid us a somewhat tearful goodbye. This time there was no curtsying, only hugs of affection, and Tracy unashamedly wept.

We were both silent in the car taking us back to Inverness airport. What we had experienced was not only satisfaction on a physical level, but also on a higher, more spiritual plane.

Tired but happy, Mr and Mrs Dawson arrived home at

Garth House, and the business of earning a living had to take over from the euphoria.

I was given a clean bill of health, but warned not to start overdoing it again.

The trouble with show business is that it never evens out – for a performer, it's either a feast or a famine.

It was now late May and I was booked to appear at the Festival Theatre in Paignton, Devon for an eight-week season with an extra week's option. Before then, I taped another series of *Blankety Blank* for the BBC, and heard that I was going to host the new series of *Opportunity Knocks*, so the future seemed rosy enough.

I was still trying to interest the public in my books, and the long haul of promotional interviews was very tiring. We rented a house with a swimming pool for the Paignton season, and it was a good job we did because it was to turn out to be one of the hottest summers imaginable.

Right from the outset, the summer season in Paignton was dogged with problems. We knew that Dana, the lovely Irish singer, was pregnant, but both my agents had been informed that her pregnancy was in the very early stages. It was therefore something of a jolt when she arrived at the theatre looking as if she was ready to give birth at any second.

Peter Goodwright and I were extremely nervous every time she walked on to the stage doing a rock medley – in fact I started the show by mentioning her condition ... not that I had to – her navel was nearer the front row than her tummy.

> *'Good evening, ladies and gentlemen, and welcome to the Festival Theatre, and believe me, you're welcome to it.... If they demolish this place they'll have to repair it first so that it's safe to pull down.'*

'As you'll notice, Dana is expecting a little event, but don't worry, in the orchestra pit we've got a set of drums and gas and air.... If anything happens, look at it this way, you get two acts for the price of one.'

Despite the jokes I was genuinely frightened in case anything did happen, and Dana agreed to the suggestion that she should cut the rock medley, which relieved me no end.

The weather, I'm afraid, kept the customers out – and who could blame them? Day after day the sun blazed from a cloudless sky, and night after night the heat drew the crowds to the shore line in order to find a breeze of sorts. During the day, Tracy and I wallowed in the swimming pool of our rented house in Torquay, and slept in the afternoon before driving to the theatre. Tragically, during the first couple of weeks of the run, Dana's father died and she left the show. Trouper that she is, she returned, but it was not for long – she left to have her baby, and I put my *Midwifery for Beginners* book away.

A funny double act came in as replacement for Dana and we continued the battle to get people in.

The double act, Diamond and Leyton, did a creditable job and it was a good show, but alas! old Sol was the ultimate victor. On the last night of the show I couldn't resist the old pro gags....

'Business has been so bad, we shot a stag last night in the balcony.'

'You can tell how bad things have been, the girl in the box had been dead a month and nobody knew.'

'A chap phoned up last week, he said "What time is the second house going up?" I said, "What time can you make it?"'

One thing that appalled me during the run of the show

was the way the Sunday concerts were billed: 'Adults only. If you are easily offended this show is not for you'. These dirty comics packed the Festival Theatre on those Sabbath nights; once again I began to have grave misgivings about the future of entertainment.

Stewart Morris, a senior BBC producer, came to see me and we discussed a series of six variety spectaculars, featuring a large orchestra and top celebrities. I was overjoyed – variety is my first love, not game shows – and I started getting material together. Despite Tracy's protests that we shouldn't get into harness so quickly, I went ahead in full agreement for the shows.

Once again we had little time to enjoy any home life as we were needed in London to put the shows together, and once again I was ignoring the advice given by the doctor: 'Slow down, take life at a slower pace. . . .' But what the hell? I felt in fine form – OK, OK, I should stop smoking, I know, but it's not so easy is it, friend?

Up and down every week on the shuttle flight between Manchester and London. . . . Every week in smoke-filled rehearsal rooms working out the stand-up comedy material and the sketches.

Finally, we staged the first programme, *The Les Dawson Show*, from the TV Centre. We had a twenty-five piece orchestra under the baton of John Coleman, John Nettles to partner me in the sketches, and, as special guest, Shirley Bassey, a superlative star who is also easy to work with. On consecutive programmes we would feature Status Quo, Elkie Brooks, David Essex, Chas and Dave, the Roly Polys, Terry Wogan. I thought the series would be a big success, but a strange programme planning decision was made: instead of waiting for the series of *Blankety Blank* to complete its run, the variety series was stuck in between the *Blankety Blank* shows.

I was devastated. The ratings for the variety shows were very poor, and indeed, when I lost my Friday night slot for *Blankety Blank* it too dropped alarmingly in popularity. It looked as if I was on my way out.

Had some august figure at the BBC declared that Dawson was to be made redundant? Had I offended someone there? Never handling money well, I was not in a position to get out of the business; saving for a rainy day was never a favourite axiom of mine, and I viewed the future with apprehension.

As the weeks went by, pantomime loomed on the horizon. This year I would be heading the bill in Sunderland, not the easiest of venues to play. Poor old Tracy was dragged away from home yet again. I knew she was growing disenchanted with show business, and some of the questionable characters we had to mix with, but I was not in any position to cease from the hurly-burly of the game. I remembered a day in the West End many years ago.... I had bumped into a man who in his day had been a star of the variety world, and I had once had the privilege of being at the bottom of a bill that he was topping. We had a drink together in a Soho pub and his eyes betrayed his hopeless situation – no longer in demand, forgotten by a newer generation, and penniless. His plight moved me very much and that night in my digs in Battersea, a small damp attic bed-sit, I wrote an essay about him. I called it simply:

THE COMEDIAN

'He stood alone on the neon-bright platform with a microphone grasped in his hand. His damp face was a mask of strain and there was an appeal for some respect in his posturing. Waiters scurried to and fro between the tables, oblivious to anything other than the shouts from the habitués of the club, as they demanded more drink to be served.

Tobacco smoke twisted into yellow garlands that then hovered around the man with the microphone, and helped to hide the despair etched in his comic delivery that nobody listened to.

... Once he had performed before a Queen; once he had shaken hands with people eager to know him, and once he had known theatrical triumphs, but now he stood before an uncaring generation, his victories unheeded. Occasionally wet-lipped faces turned in his direction, only to sullenly return to bury the indifference into a brimming tankard; other faces broke into sneers at the comedy man, and other faces laughed at him ... not with him. The sweat glistened on his brow and the heavy stage make-up ran in rills to confuse the colour of his frayed shirt collar. He raised his voice in an effort to be heard, but the microphone system merely whistled and grated and he lost his timing to a howl of obscenities.... Once he had performed before a Queen, and once he had shaken hands with people eager to know him. But that was a long time ago, wasn't it?

The three-piece band bludgeoned his play-off music into a dreadful parody of harmony and he mustered one last desperate smile. To his tormentors he bowed in surrender, then walked off the rostrum.

He shrugged off the loud check jacket in the cramped cubicle that passed as a dressing-room, removed the tarnished make-up of illusion, and in the mirror his eyes reflected his inner sense of failure.

He would sit in that dressing-room until the club emptied, then he would creep away to the cheap accommodation where he could lie and remember the way it was.... Once he had performed before a Queen, and once he had shaken hands with people who had been eager to know him....

Tomorrow he would go and stand on the stage of another club, and perhaps there, somebody would remember him.'

* * *

I think that man did more to help me keep my feet on the ground than any other person. During a success, I would recall his aged and wistful face and my heart would go out to his memory, for soon after our drink together in that Soho pub, he gassed himself in his cold, comfortless flat in Notting Hill Gate.

I found myself remembering him more often as the critics attacked some of my television appearances. The six variety shows, although reviewed warmly in the more august newspapers, received poor notices in the tabloids, and I felt my popularity was on the wane.

The feeling grew when the advance bookings for the Sunderland pantomime, *Jack and the Beanstalk*, were sent through to my agents' office – it was a very lukewarm advance, to say the least.

In fact it wasn't a bad pantomime, but it lacked the glitter and imagination to draw the public in to see it. I got the feeling that the production had been conceived in a burning desire to see how cheaply it could be staged. Some of the scenery loooked as if it had once graced a Second World War ENSA concert. The whole thing smacked of accountancy; in my view that is what went wrong with show business: the takeover of entertainment by accountants. Accountants are good with figures but not with people. Accountants can look after the finances of a company but not run a company. As a result, the Sunderland pantomime season was not a memorable one.

Along the way I had another brush with the press. I gave interviews quite freely to all the media, and during one such interview, this time with a local newspaper, the journalist asked me what was the most expensive present that I had ever bought Tracy. As we drank a Scotch or two, I said that it was probably her engagement ring. He then asked if Tracy had a fur coat. I said yes, she'd had one for quite some time actually, but I think the writer got the impression that it had been bought recently as a Christmas gift. He asked me if I agreed with women wearing furs. I replied that freedom of choice was the prerequisite of democracy, and in my view man-made fabrics were probably causing more harm to the environment than the use of natural skins.... That did it! Two days later the national press got hold of the story, animal rights demonstrators paraded past the theatre with makeshift banners, and the headlines read: 'Dawson believes in killing the mink'. Naturally the public had to be reminded that I was married to an ex-barmaid and that my wife had only been dead just under three years before I remarried, so I felt like a cross between a Kenyan poacher and Bluebeard. The nice thing about the people of Sunderland was the fact that in their view I could buy the wife anything I wanted – provided I didn't abuse whippets and racing pigeons!

Everybody in show business rang me up asking how the hell I managed to get into so much trouble and so often!

Once before, while on tour with *Run For Your Wife*, I was interviewed in the Theatre Royal, Bath. A local reporter asked me what I thought of the prizes on *Blankety Blank*. Casually I had said that they were rubbish, but that was the good thing about the game show ... greed wasn't the motive for taking part in it. Innocent? The national press picked up the remark, and the headlines boomed jovially: 'Dawson Calls It Blankety Junk' and '*Blankety Blank* is rubbish, says Dawson'.

What made me chuckle about the incident was that on every *Blankety Blank* I told the world at large that the prizes were crap.... Well, how else could you describe them? One chap from Arbroath won a garden ornament.... It turned out to be a peculiar looking tulip in a plastic sort of birdcage.

However, my stock certainly didn't go up at the BBC, I'm sad to say.

The pantomime thankfully limped to its conclusion, and Tracy and I beetled off home. More work followed on my next book, a parody of Raymond Chandler's famous thriller, *Farewell My Lovely.* Tracy begged me to relax, then, when I ignored her plea she turned nasty and dragged me off to Tenerife.

We had delays at Manchester Airport, we had delays at London Heathrow, then more delays at Madrid Airport, closely followed by a longer delay at another airport that turned out to be a sort of Spanish Biggin Hill – they even still had a poster of Franco up in the lounge. The imp had struck again. This time the little sod contrived to lose my luggage *and* my passport.... But, ha ha! I found the blessed passport in the lavatory, it had dropped out of my pants pocket whilst I was in the throes of straining with a tummy bug.... Oh yes, I had acute diarrhoea. I had time to jot down an impression of an airport....

> Faces in a hurry everywhere... anxious faces; troubled faces, faces serene with anticipation and faces with a moisture of stress bobbing in confused masses amongst the mountains of leather containers that await destination labels to be affixed on them by robotic employees behind airline plinths.
>
> Strangled voices from loudspeakers grate forth inaudible instructions to a descant of clattering feet that are making towards the hum of the escalators.
>
> There are travellers with noses pressed into magazines and newspapers, there are people sitting with hot children loudly mewing for attention, and there are people with vacancies in their eyes, watching the silver mammoths soaring down the runway....

Priests in clutches shuffle in piety among the holidaymakers and taut business executives and tone down the colourful parade in black cloths of indifferent humility.

A cacophony of sound rises towards the high centre dome, and creates a discordant chant against the drumming of mighty engines as the eager crowds surge for the departure lounges.... The rank odour of body heat clashes with pungent perfumes, and the reek of tobaccos, as the shouldering mass scurry sightless to the check-in points ... each gripping cards of permission for sonic propulsion to far pavilions.

A stewardess behind a practised mask, which now lengthens into a smiling line, ushers her charges to cramped confinement, soothing their fears with trim uniformed authority.

Tardy arrivals with aching lungs edge into the aero tube and promote glares from long-seated passengers.

Suddenly, the structure shudders and the whine of the mechanism stills desultory conversation as the unknown beckons a spectre'd invitation to a nation of cloud and an alien horizon.

Although I enjoyed the challenge of penning the essay with descriptive language, it still didn't get rid of the fact that my luggage was missing and that my bowels were in full rebellion.... So much for bloody holidays. Fortunately, the weather in Tenerife was truly magnificent and for ten days and nights Tracy and I slept, swam, and made love, then ate and drank, and slept some more. Two days later my suitcase arrived looking as if it had been sat on by a horse.

Apart from an odd chap who tried to sell me a villa on a cliff and then ran away when a police car hove into view, it was a relaxing holiday, but looking at my spreading girth and listening to my wheezy chest, I made a mental note to go for a check-up when I got home. Tracy was distressed by the number of cigarettes I was smoking, and I was drinking more than was good for me ... and she still couldn't get me to have an early night. Would I ever learn?

Uphill and Downhill

People saw the familiar little figure glowing with happiness as he proudly accompanied his beautiful young wife on business and social occasions.

They saw her laugh at his endless jokes, but when he pattered on about show business....

'I'm booked here tonight, I have another gig next April and possibly one for late November.... They're not just engagements – the way things are going, that's a career.'

'I'm not saying the business was bad at the theatre, but during my act, there were so many empty seats, monks walked through on the way to vespers.'

'People often ask me what is the difference between a Northern audience and a Southern audience when it comes to comedy ... I've found no difference, they don't laugh at me in the South either.'

They couldn't see the anxiety in his mind, as the engagements started to dry up....

Bronzed and rested, we arrived back home with just enough time to unpack the holiday gear, then repack our cases for the trip to London, where I was hosting the new series of *Opportunity Knocks*. The series was shot at Elstree Studios, and I thought it had a lot of merit.

We desperately need to promote new talent in this country, and I thought we did one hell of a good job doing just that on *Opportunity Knocks*. So what went wrong? I've asked myself that time and again. The set for the aspiring performers was quite awe-inspiring, and once again John Coleman led a huge orchestra to back the raw artistes. Maybe that was the problem, perhaps it was too overwhelming for a new-to-television performer ... I don't know.

I worked hard to make the series succeed but when it was shown, the ratings were poor and I began to think that I was past my peak and all washed up.

The critics were not kind either to me or to the young hopefuls, and it made me angry that these eager newcomers should have to read the cruel things some individuals wrote about them. For myself, I was used to being knocked about by the media. There seems to be an odd quirk in the British character, which is we're not comfortable with success. Success bothers us somehow, and once somebody has attained a high degree of it, we immediately attempt to destroy it.

One thing was for sure, whatever part the press had played in the past to give my career a boost, it had now changed direction and appeared to be doing a demolition job on me.... Whatever I did was wrong.

I felt that I was letting the young hopefuls down, and yet despite the poor ratings for each weekly show, when it came to the live transmission of the grand finale to see who was the outright winner, that particular programme shot up in the ratings and my spirits soared.

When *Opportunity Knocks* ended its run – with the promise of another series – Tracy and I had but a short time before setting forth on another tour of *Run For Your Wife*. We needed a break and we decided to join my agents on a four-day business trip to New York. Tracy was bubbling with excitement and I caught some of her enthusiasm.

We took an ordinary flight out to Kennedy Airport, seven hours of boredom and fitful dozing, at least for me, but Tracy was a child again, peering through the glass at the cloud formations ... it was a joy to see her complete enthusiasm.

The first thing that struck me about New York was the politeness of everybody! The last time I had visited the States rudeness was the vogue from the airport officials to the hotel staff. This time, however, people smiled at us at Kennedy, a civil porter helped me out with the luggage to a taxi rank, and by all that is holy, the taxi driver was politeness personified. Naturally, like every other cabbie in New York he had absolutely no idea where he was going and his knowledge of New York would have fitted with room to spare in a flea's truss. However, despite the warfare of the rush hour traffic, he managed to get us to the Halloran Hotel (now the Marriott) on Lexington Avenue.

I took Tracy to the theatres on Broadway, we lunched at Lindy's, held hands in Times Square, gasped as we looked down from the top of the Empire State Building, and loved the narrow streets of Greenwich Village. We cantered through Central Park in a horse-drawn surrey and drank cocktails in dimly-lit Fifth Avenue bars.... All too soon, Tracy and I returned home again to face the future and what it held for us.

Just prior to the *Run For Your Wife* tour, I had a visit from a very concerned, high-ranking policeman who informed us that it appeared there had been a death threat made against me. As you can imagine, this news caused me to shake like a plate of junket. I'm no hero, but I'll face an enemy on a one-to-one basis – but when you are seriously told that someone has threatened to shoot you – well, it's not very nice, I can assure you.

At first I was tempted to treat the incident as a hoax, but the police insisted that they had proof that the threat was real. That snippet of news sent me straight to the loo for an emergency evacuation.

For weeks after, I watched out for strangers everywhere; a pheasant cackling to itself on my lawn must have thought the world had come to an end when a sad-faced, portly comedian lunged in its direction brandishing a bread knife and yelling, 'Face me, you cowardly bastard.'

I even considered wearing a disguise to fool the would-be assassin, but Tracy said her dresses wouldn't fit me.... It was quite a while before the sensation of being a hunted animal wore off.

I did a number of telly shots, guesting on other people's shows: Bruce Forsyth and Noel Edmonds, Terry Wogan and Gloria Hunniford, and the shots went well but the money was a joke. On Terry's chat show I said to him that I always took the BBC cheque I got for appearing on *Wogan* straight to the bank when I received it, mainly because it was too small to go on its own.

Run For Your Wife opened in Cardiff and bloody near closed there.... The business was disappointing and the cast – Peter Goodwright, Gordon Honeycombe, Maurice Thoroughgood, Brian Godfrey, Jilly Foote and Jan Hunt – battled against indifference, and a heatwave (it was a summer tour).

Despite glowing reviews in all the local newspapers the business didn't pick up. I blamed a lot of it on my lack of pulling power these days – in truth, I'd noticed that the volume of fan mail I was sent was beginning to dwindle.

From Cardiff we played Swansea, only marginally better trade. Wolverhampton turned out better than we had expected, as did Leeds and Nottingham, but Hull wasn't going to be a record breaker. However, our bacon was retrieved in Newcastle at the Theatre Royal. I like that part of the world – I love the wild Northumbrian coast; the ghosts of Vikings haunt the castles and the dashing cliffs, and the sea on that coast is always turbulent and threatening. . . .

My elder daughter, Julie, and her fiancé set the date for their wedding during the tour of the play, which meant that the ceremony had to be held on a Sunday in order for Tracy and me to be able to attend. Once again, father's hand dipped deep into his linings . . . ah well! This time I sincerely hoped that the wedding would go ahead; the year before she had nearly made the altar with another young man, but with just a few days to go she had seen the error of her ways and cancelled the whole thing. I need not have concerned myself: this time she wed her childhood sweetheart, John, the sun shone, and it went off swimmingly. I could have been forgiven, surely, for getting plastered? After all, it's not every day that you surrender your daughter to another man, is it? Alone together in the house, just before she set off for the church with her proud father, Julie walked down the stairs, and my heart skipped a beat . . . for it was like looking at her mother on her wedding day. . . . I held Julie close, and said the things that all fathers say, but I felt a sense of loss. My firstborn. . . .

Once more the curtains of time had been drawn back . . . there she is, lying in the cot next to Meg . . . is she really part of me, that tiny sleeping bundle? Is that my daughter going to school for the first time? Is that me wiping her tears as she clings to me at the school gate? Why do the years have to rush by so madly.... Stop, let me talk to that young girl just in her tormented teens, it's Julie, isn't it? Now she's a bride and I'm losing her.... Why, oh why, God, couldn't you have let my Meg see her daughter married before you took her away?

Julie looked radiant in the church, and a glow surrounded her and her husband as the two of them stood before the altar....

After the ceremony I needed to be alone and I took myself off into the old churchyard. It had rained the night before and tendrils of ground mist drifted over the moist soil and the surfaces of long forgotten tombstones. I stood and smoked a cigarette, and thought about all the dreams and desires buried along with the bones of the dead. How pointless is the pursuit of immortality when all must come to this....

I threw away the cigarette as I heard my name being called, and retraced my steps through the coarse grass strangling the bases of the burial monoliths, brushed aside the hanging branches of uncared-for trees, and rejoined the happy scene upon the lawn outside the church door.

We had two weeks left of the tour after Julie's marriage and as always, when the play ended its run, I wished it could go on much longer. In show business, you come together in a production, often as strangers, but as time goes by you become a family, and it's a wrench when you have to part.

So little time... September now... in a few short weeks pantomime again! Tracy shook her head in despair at our workload, but she did all she could to prepare for yet another long run. This year the pantomime was to be *Dick Whittington* at the Palace Theatre, Manchester.

It was at the press call held in the circle bar of the Palace Theatre that my forebodings about my future took on a more ominous reality. Over drinks I faced a huge assembly of reporters and photographers.... I waited for questions about the format of the pantomime to be directed at me. The first question shook me rigid: 'Afternoon, Les, I want to ask you, how does it feel to have both your television shows dropped?'

I looked at the pressman ... he'd certainly pulled the rug from under my feet, because nobody at the BBC had said anything about dumping me, either to me or my agent. Yet this reporter knew, and I knew it was the truth by the steady gaze he directed at me. I felt as though I'd been kicked by a mule. Both my shows axed and not a word to me about it.... I couldn't believe such discourtesy. For over five years I had hosted *Blankety Blank* on a very successful basis, and now no more, just like that. Somehow I parried his question but the other newshounds took up the hue and cry. Not one of them appeared interested in the current panto production, only in my downfall.

After the press call and that bombshell, I was very dispirited indeed. Dear Tracy consoled me and I knew that she was more important than a television show, but I was hurt. Oh, I knew that the signs had been around for some time ... dwindling fan mail, less interest – indifference even – if I was spotted in the street; was I over the hill?

At least I had some work ahead in the shape of the panto, but what worried me now was, would I be able to pull the crowds in with my name? Being virtually sacked from two major productions presumably because of poor viewing figures was not exactly a recommendation, and I confess I was worried.

Tracy was mad at my attitude.

'What is the matter with you?' she railed at me when she got fed up with my self-pity. 'You've been at the top for longer than most, it won't do you any harm to sit back and allow us both to have some home life. I don't think being top in the flaming ratings is all that important to be honest – health and someone to care for are more important.' With that she cried on my shoulder and I knew that I was behaving like a bloody fool. Tracy was so right; why did I keep forgetting the lessons I should have learnt from the past?

God had given me another chance, and another love in my life, and like an idiot, instead of being eternally grateful, I was back to being the selfish, ambitious twit who had twice put himself at the doors of death because of his overriding ego. There and then I decided to try to be halfway intelligent and to be grateful for what I had achieved and now possessed. I felt better, and when yet another reporter buttonholed me and crowed about my losing two shows, I cheerfully said yes, it was true, no, I wasn't upset, after all I was merely employed by the BBC and if they'd had enough of me, then that was their prerogative. No, I wasn't upset – of course you can print that, I said, and the reporter hurried away in an exalted state.

Two days later the feature came out and the newspaper printed what I'd said – which was a change – but the article made me sound as if I was on the bottom line with no hope and hated by everybody from the head of the Beeb to the janitor in the cellar.

My agent rang up, furious (which he frequently was,

and still is) with me. 'Dolly' (his favourite mode of address), 'will you stop talking to the newspapers,' he boomed down the line. 'You are talking a load of cock and it just might interest you to know that the advance booking at the Palace Theatre Manchester for the panto, *with you top of the bill*, has already broken every existing record. So nobody wants you, hey dolly?'

Good old Norman ... my flagging morale rose like an eagle! I embraced Tracy, then saw the look in her eye and remembered to be humble and satisfied with the way things were right now. The news of the solid advance for the pantomime was simply a bonus.

Before rehearsals for the pantomime began in London, Tracy and I had time to be alone together, and with her encouragment I started writing descriptive essays.

It became a habit of mine to take long walks and carry a notebook with me in order to jot down descriptions of what I saw, and now that I was taking things more easily I found I was enjoying things I'd never had time to notice before. Sitting quietly in my garden, for instance, with only the sound of the waterfall giggling into my fish pond, I suddenly noticed a squirrel ambling around. I watched birds swoop and trill and a stoat chasing a rabbit across the conifer bed – these things were happening all around me, in my own backyard – why hadn't I seen all this before?

Opening night at the Palace Theatre, Manchester was a triumph. John Nettles, the Roly Polys, Anne Sydney, Mark Walker and I took curtain after curtain, and the show was a guaranteed success with the biggest advance in the history of the theatre. Despite 'bugs' laying low half the cast during our ten-week run, we never played to less than a full house, even when we lost John Nettles for three weeks with a flu virus.

All the children had tummy problems; it was just as well the audience could not see them throwing up in the many buckets arranged in the wings. I was lucky that season, I only had my customary bowel infection, double pneumonia and yellow fever, so I was able to totter on every night and perform.

Whilst in Manchester the BBC approached me with an idea for a game show entitled *Fast Friends*. Ah, if only I could have foreseen the consequences.

I left Manchester flushed with triumph. We'd taken so much money, we'd received such wonderful reviews, I was ten and a half feet tall. After a brief few weeks at home, I signed to do *Fast Friends*, and Tracy and I began our weekly flights to London, and then on to Elstree to record what will probably be known in years to come as the greatest load of crap ever to be committed to film as far as I was concerned.

The show was an American idea and it should have stayed right there in America – preferably on Boot Hill. I've dropped some big ones in my time, but agreeing to do that show was akin to heaving an elephant's testicles down a pit shaft.

From the moment we discussed it, trouble wafted in. My own opinion was that of all the game shows imported from the States, *Fast Friends* was the most American. Its whole premise rested on the antics of crackpot contestants almost wetting themselves in their excitement, and our American cousins seem to excel at producing this type of inanity.

My agents hated the whole concept from day one, but the BBC begged and pleaded with us to carry on with the project. There then commenced a series of furious arguments of a kind not heard outside the United Nations, and people would stalk off muttering things. It was quite ridiculous.

Rehearsals were full of the sort of happy anticipation usually associated with a grave robber's lunch break ... and nothing went right. Behind me on the platform built on the studio floor was a sort of screen with a string of lights in a semicircle over the top. The contestants sat slightly below me, divided into teams, and each team had to select a team leader, who then pranced on to the rostrum with me, one on each side. I now asked one of them to pick a member of his or her team to answer a question, while the string of lights above me clicked off the number of seconds it took the team member to answer. (Have you got it? Good, because I couldn't get the hang of the wretched game, and tempers began to fray.)

I don't think the first programme will ever be forgotten by those who suffered through it, but they say that time is a great healer. For a start, the company who had sold the game show to the Beeb had brought in what can almost be described as 'professional contestants'. They knew more about game shows than we did. They very nearly took over the show, and the studio audience sat with their mouths agape watching the battle royal taking place before them ... it was one hell of a punch-up. At one stage the contestants surrounded the Head of Variety and the poor devil had virtually to be rescued by armed police!

Eventually, after one attempt to film the epic, we contrived, with the aid of garlic posies and a crucifix, to shoot one show which was appalling. I got rid of some of the 'professional contestants' and brought several of the studio audience in as replacements and we did the show again. It was about as enjoyable as watching the slaughter of a bullock; to make matters worse, the replacements were heckled by the original contestants, at least one of whom was blotto.

After the débâcle, we all sat around a table in the bar in a silence reminiscent of that of a long-forgotten tomb. But we were committed: the series was to go ahead. I ignored the good advice offered to me – such as emigrating or committing suicide or becoming a Trappist monk. The rest is history, I suppose. Suffice to say the series didn't make any waves on the network. It didn't even make a plop.

The reviews were all ghastly, the ratings were so low the only people who watched it lived in a submarine, and frankly *Fast Friends* put a man-sized nail in my theatrical coffin.

Tracy, supportive as always, said, 'The show was no worse than some of the others they put out,' and to a degree she was right. The trouble was, it was too American for British audiences, and that is all I'm prepared to say without a cheap lawyer around, if there is such a thing.

We returned home from Elstree after canning the series and I wanted to go into immediate hiding, but Tracy pulled me out of the coal cellar. Not only did my fan mail dry up after the screening of *Fast Friends* but the telephone practically stopped ringing and I began to understand the isolation felt by Robinson Crusoe. I had had no offers for a summer season – nobody seemed to want me. Up to a point I wasn't too bothered; Tracy and I needed to do a lot to the house and we welcomed the chance to catch up on some social life, but the thought of being rejected by the business did hurt, I must say.

Actually, I had been offered Bournemouth Pier for eight weeks to star in a play called *Boeing Boeing*, but I felt bound to turn it down – it just wasn't my cup of tea. The leading character is suave and sophisticated, and that I ain't.

So the rest of the year yawned in front of us with little work in prospect, a belligerent tax inspector in the wings, a heap of bills the size of an average Alp on my desk, and a hefty overdraft at the bank.

Fortunately Norman and Anne came through as sort of bagel-chewing Messiahs with a commercial to do for the Post Office. I was to supply the voices of two old women gossiping about the benefits of using your local Post Office.

I worked on the ad with a bright young team, and I like to think it is now regarded as a little masterpiece. It was especially welcome to me, because it gave me a chance to bring to life Cissie and Ada, the two characters I'd created for television, with Roy Barraclough as Cissie. Because variety was finished, and because Roy was under sole contract to *Coronation Street*, the two characters had disappeared from the TV screens, which was sad, because they had been a source of enjoyment to many people. I can still recall the first script I ever wrote for the two elderly windbags, back in 1975 on Yorkshire Television's *Sez Les*. There had been some doubts about audience reaction to a pair of old ladies being a bit vulgar, but we needn't have worried on that score.

CISSIE: Hello, chuck, Leonard and I have been on holiday … in Greece.

ADA: Very nice. Actually Bert and me went to Greece once with Peabody's Inter-Continental Floral Tours, on HP.

CISSIE: Really? Tell me, did you have the shish kebabs there?

ADA: From the moment we got there.… Bert said it was the warm beer that did it.

CISSIE: You really are pig ignorant, Ada.... Did you see the Acropolis?

ADA: See it? We were never off the damn thing. Bert had to wear rubber pants to stop the chafing.

CISSIE: Leonard took some lovely photos ... he's got a big Polaroid.

ADA: Ooh, they can be painful, does it affect his balance?

CISSIE: I don't know why I bother with you, Ada. Compared to your Bert my Leonard is a saint. In all things he is most circumspect.

ADA: I never knew he was Jewish.

CISSIE: Oh, you are impossible. Anyway, I can't stop, I'm going to see Mrs Scattergood, she's the spiritualist from Acker Street, she talks to the spirit world.

ADA: She talks to dead people? I'll have to get her to have a word with my Bert ... he's been lifeless for years. We haven't performed....

CISSIE: I don't wish to know about you and Bert doing that. Mrs Scattergood gets in touch with the spirits through her ouija.

ADA: Oh my God....

CISSIE: She often goes into a trance.

ADA: If she's talking through her ouija, it's a wonder she doesn't get severe cramp.

CISSIE: Very good is Mrs Scattergood, and her husband has a crystal ball.

ADA: Marvellous what they can do today.

CISSIE: He was a prisoner of war in Singapore. The Japanese caught him after he was cut off from his Chindits.

ADA: I often wondered why they had no kids.

The audience howled at the tongue-in-cheek vulgarity, none more so than the middle-aged ladies among them. Cissie and Ada were to live on television for over fourteen years, and not one letter of complaint was ever sent in.

The two characters epitomised those wonderful

women of the Lancashire mill towns who, because of the noise of the looms, had to become expert lip-readers in order to communicate with each other. Now, thanks to the Post Office, I could make them live again ... all was not lost, was it?

That summer Tracy and I were invited to 10 Downing Street to meet John Major: it was a memorable occasion. There were many artistes and professional people gathered there, but Mr Major and his wife had time to give to every single individual present.

After my umpteenth glass of champagne I decided to tell the Prime Minister, who'd come over to talk to us, how to run the country. His handshake was firm and he looked me squarely in the eye, which let's face it, is unusual for a politician.

'Mr Major,' I boomed as I swayed, 'in my considered opinion, the only way to restore this country's economy is to lower income tax at the direct level to less than 20%, then scrap VAT altogether and in its place introduce indirect taxation. This will stop the envy between the haves and the have-nots, and when people have more money to spend at the source of their income I feel that they will go out into the High Street and spend much more.'

I sensed that Mr Major was trying to get away and Tracy was pinching my arm, but nothing – do you hear? *nothing* – was going to halt the flow of my inspired rhetoric, no sirree.

'The next thing to do, Mr Major,' said I with a perceptible burp, 'is to scrap company tax for the first year on a new enterprise, then impose only half company tax during the second year, and full tax on the third year, thus enabling a business to amass a cash flow. As regards the

Common Market, tell 'em to get knotted and woo the Empire back. There is still no diplomacy like gunboat diplomacy....'

On and on I went until I ran out of ideas. Mr Major looked at me. I half expected him to grab me by the shoulders, plant an ecstatic kiss on each cheek, turn to the assembly and shout: 'Hail to Britain's saviour'.... Instead he said, 'Les, you look after the laughs and I'll look after the money.' So ended my stab at a career in politics.

The following afternoon– a glorious one – Tracy and I, togged out in our finery, went to Buckingham Palace for one of the annual Garden Parties. We walked around, feeling so elegant, waving to people, signing autographs, sipping tea and primly chewing cucumber sandwiches. I couldn't help wondering what my mother and father would have said if they could have seen their ragamuffin son strolling around Buck House.... All they had ever known was grinding poverty and a constant struggle to survive.

I saw again the mean back streets and the haunted look on the faces of those who lived in the grim two-up and two-downs ... and yet, despite the lack of material possessions, my parents had given me so much love that I had the confidence to walk among kings with my head held high.

As we chatted, Prince Philip, in his immaculate grey tails, came striding across the manicured lawns towards our marquee and the crowd hushed. To my astonishment he suddenly shouted out: 'Where's Dawson? I want to speak to Dawson.' The crowd gasped, and Tracy blushed with pride. His Royal Highness shook my hand warmly and Tracy dimpled attractively when the Prince held her hand and smiled. We chatted, and before long the subject of black puddings cropped up yet again. Before we go any further I'd better explain the black-pudding saga.

Some years ago at a club in Luton, I compered a big Variety show that was televised before Prince Philip. The two-hour programme starred among others, the Drifters, Peters and Lee, the Peter Gordeno Dancers and Charlie Smithers, and was in aid of charity.

Afterwards the Prince was escorted to a room to meet local dignitaries and the organisers of the show. I'd found my way to the bar – the drinks were free that evening, and I didn't want them to think they'd gone to all that trouble for nothing, so I started to demolish a few large ones. Suddenly I heard Prince Philip's voice: 'Where's Dawson?' I turned and saw him striding towards me. We shook hands and he asked for a beer, then he proceeded to say how much he'd enjoyed the show and so forth. 'Are you still living in the North?' he asked. I nodded and he went on to say how much he had enjoyed a visit to Rochdale with Her Majesty the Queen, in order to open a shopping centre. 'Nice people up there,' he said. 'They presented us with some black-puddings, you know. Absolutely delicious, had 'em fried for breakfast.' I don't know what possessed me to say it, but I did: 'Actually, sir, you really should boil them, that's the traditional Northern way.'

His Royal Highness stared at me with a twinkle in his eye and replied: 'Absolute rubbish, Dawson, you fry 'em.'

I almost forgot who I was talking to. 'You boil the damn things, I should know,' I spluttered back.

'Rot ... they have to be fried.'

'Typical Southern trick – you're supposed to boil the buggers.'

Suddenly I became aware that several gentlemen of the press were edging closer, presumably to hear what was going on, and we finished our argument about the estimable puddings on a good-humoured note. Ever since then, whenever I have met the Prince, the dialogue about black puddings is continued, and this particular afternoon under a blazing sun in the gardens of Buckingham Palace was no exception.

PRINCE PHILIP: Did you enjoy the buffet provided?
LITTLE ME: Very nice, sir. Pity there were no black puddings, though.
PRINCE PHILIP: If they had been provided, Dawson, I would have made quite sure that they were fried.

Well, he is the Prince, so I let him have the last line!

One day I was asked to speak at a big charity dinner hosted by Prince Edward at St James's Palace, and of course I readily accepted. I was curious to see inside the Palace, whose very walls speak history and countless years of pageantry and tradition . . . what's that wonderful Blimp phrase again? 'Any man born an Englishman has won the first prize in the lottery of life'.

A good friend of ours, dressed in the garb of an upper-class chauffeur, drove us down the Mall and straight into the forecourt of the Palace, and Tracy and I drifted through the portals of the historical pile, our noses so high in the air our nostrils looked like sunglasses! A rather long, toothy sort of chap welcomed us into a reception area and guided us to a table crowded with bottles of champagne, and we began to sample the grape.

Every chap there seemed long and toothy. The ladies present were gowned magnificently, and they too were long and toothy.

'Aren't you the comedian chappie?' said one precious type with a monocle in a bloodshot eye.

Another haughty 'I'm a Guards officer, don't yer know' type asked me if I'd served in the forces at all. The way in which he asked the question made me suspect that he rather thought I hadn't, or if I had, perhaps the Pioneer Corps had claimed me. I drew myself up proudly, because I did have the distinction of doing my National Service in one of the Army's most famous old regiments, The Queen's Bays, 2nd Dragoon Guards. Yes, a cavalry regiment, by thunder! When I loftily informed the gentleman of this notable fact, I sensed a faint glimmer of respect.... The fact that I never amounted to a row of beans in the service, or that I was twice nearly court-martialled (once for being Brahms and Liszt on sentry duty), or that I tried to work my ticket out of the Army, I didn't think worth mentioning at the time. Suffice to say The Queen's Bays, 2nd Dragoon Guards is a great title to pose under.

Meanwhile the reception area was filling up with the Top People. By this time I was flushed with wine, dying for a pee, and choking for a cigarette, but there were 'No Smoking' signs in evidence and the long, toothy men and women didn't look like smokers. However, to me, being without the Weed is a torment akin to the disappointment of a hedgehog discovering that it's been trying to mount a Brillo pad.

I snapped. Excusing myself from the knot of gentlefolk who were engaging us in conversation, I tootled into the ornate lav, peed mightily like a shire horse, and then addressed myself to the long and toothy gentlemen crammed in the ancient loo. 'Excuse me, chaps,' I almost shouted, 'I hope I don't offend anybody but I simply must have a cigarette.' Instead of protests, a relieved cry went up: 'THANK GOD ... WELL DONE, DAWSON!' We all lit up, puffed little clouds into the air – we were friends ... buddies ... comrades.

Sated with nicotine, I waltzed back to Tracy and downed several more glasses of champagne. By now everybody was my pal and I wasn't seeing too clearly. At some sort of summons we were all ushered towards a door, through which we trooped into the beautiful Throne Room. Row upon row of red plush, ormolu chairs awaited us, for we were to be entertained by that fine young violinist Nigel Kennedy, he of the punk look and neck rash to match. I sat next to Prince Edward with Tracy on my left, in the front row. It was hot, and the drink was causing my attention to wander. I'm told that I leered at the women and bared my fillings and winked at the gentlemen.

Now, Nigel Kennedy is a superlative musician and there are times when I positively thirst for Vivaldi ... but after forty minutes of it in a hot, musty chamber with a tum full of champers, my eyes were beginning to worm their way out of their sockets. My eyelids welded together, and I slumped against Prince Edward's shoulder.

He pushed me back upright. After a decent pause, I glazed over once more and slumped back on the Royal shoulder – this time, so Tracy assures me, with a blubbery snore. By some sort of mercy in heaven, Nigel and Vivaldi ground to a halt, and it was now time to be ushered into yet another historic chamber for the Charity Dinner.

Prince Edward looked at me as if I was pinned under a microscope and said to a rather grim Tracy: 'Does he always do that?'

We sat with Prince Edward at the top table, our fellow diners consisting of an admiral, the head of British Telecom, two sun-bleached American ladies, and a millionaire. The food was excellent and the wine superb, and even I realised that I was getting quite drunk, and I still had to speak before this glittering assembly.

Prince Edward spoke first after the coffee, and he was both erudite and funny. I felt a twinge of apprehension creep through the booze.

The Prince went down a storm and did my old eyes deceive me, or was there a triumphant look of 'Follow that' about the smile on his face? I got gingerly to my feet, aided by Tracy's grip on my arm. Behind Prince Edward hung an oil painting of enormous dimensions, a family portrait of the saddest bunch of people I've ever seen ... dark, miserable royals of long ago.... I had my opening.

'Good evening, ladies and gentlemen. On the wall behind His Royal Highness you will see a painting of a family – and by the look of them I'd say they've just sat through a rendering of Vivaldi by Nigel Kennedy.'

Thank God, the line brought the house down and Nigel Kennedy, bless him, was the first to laugh.

I had a ball that night; I called St James's Palace the 'first council house'; I ribbed the guests and the Prince; even Tracy came under attack....

'I was sat in the garden the other night, reading my marriage certificate – I was looking for a loophole.'

'The wife and I have a wonderful relationship – she does things her way and I do things her way.'

'Alas, the wife's had to give her job up. She's got rheumatism in her shoulder and can't throw the harpoon properly.'

I finished the speech on a cheeky note:

'Well, what can I say about being here with you all here tonight? Simply that I envy me feet – they've been asleep longer than I have.'

The evening ended with me being laid to snore on the back seat of our car, and I have a dim memory of Tracy getting me in an armlock as she shoved me into bed.

It was only as dawn's bars of light lunged into the bedroom that I realised that I had blown any chance of a medal or an honour – in fact, I half expected a summons to the Tower!

Some months before, I had been sent the manuscript of a play by Roberto Cossa entitled *La Nona*. This means 'The Old One' in Spanish, and was just about the weirdest piece I had ever perused.

Basically, it was an indictment of inflation and its effects on society. Set in Argentina, *La Nona* is about a hundred-year-old woman who does nothing but eat all day and all night, while her family have to work and toil just to feed her. *La Nona* is, of course, inflation, which eats into every corner of society until it destroys it. It was one hell of a challenge. I agreed to play the title role – the old woman, 'La Nona'.

Tracy thought it was a good idea and my agent said, 'There's one thing about it, if you're playing a hundred-year-old woman, it won't take long to make you up for the part.' Sometimes I have dark thoughts about my agent....

We rehearsed in London for three weeks and I learnt a lot from the marvellous cast which was comprised of Maurice Denham, Liz Smith, Jim Broadbent, Tim Snell, Jane Horrocks and Susan Binum. We shot the play in the BBC studios in Birmingham, and the experience of working up the script from mere words into a filmed project was for me sensational. I rate it one of the best things I have ever done, and although it stunned public and critics alike, I think in later years it will be seen as a little masterpiece.

La Nona was given a press review in London. Tracy and I laughed and joked a lot, but inside I was seething, because after the showing of the film – which drew rapturous applause from the audience – all the press wanted to know was how much weight I had put on because of having to eat vast quantities of food in every scene. Typical, of course, but irritating. The truth of the matter is, I don't think the press had much idea what the play was all about.

BBC2 took a chance showing *La Nona*. Although it failed to get monster ratings (the present day God of television, alas!), many discerning viewers wrote in to say how much they'd enjoyed it.

My new book, *Well Fared, My Lovely,* was due to come out, which meant trotting round to help promote it, and Tracy and I prepared for the tour. First, though, we had been invited to the Isle of Man by the friends whose wedding gift to us had been that dreamlike honeymoon in the Scottish castle. We'd been invited aboard a sailing ship sponsored by the Polish Government, and indeed the entire crew were Polish cadets. It was the most beautiful sight as it lay in the harbour at Douglas. The three giant masts, stretching up through the heavens, vibrated with the weight of the vast, billowing white sails.

The sun shone down as we crossed the gangplank on to the well-scrubbed deck, where a reception awaited us: bottles of chilled wine, and turkey legs with scoops of caviare.... I raised my fists to the gods above: 'Nothing can go wrong with this excursion,' I crowed.

The majestic clipper thrust its prow through the

breasting waves, and only a slight judder indicated our passage from the harbour. We drank and nibbled, and the conversation sparkled. I watched the gallant Polish cadets climbing the rigging, up and up, like a host of feverish primates, holding on to spars and ropes as the strengthening wind pulled and tugged their clothing. Down went the wine and out came the wit and repartee as I stood with the captain on the bridge, but jokes in Polish don't sound as funny as they do when told in West Hartlepool.

Douglas was no longer in sight ... no land was visible as we rose and fell through the quickening sea. Balancing became a problem as the towering waves rose into white peaks. Passengers caught in a wind eddy suddenly started to spin like so many toy tops, and playful rollers threw curtains of numbing seawater over the decks. The wine and turkey had by now formed an alliance in my stomach to torment me into vomiting my greed overboard, and in this action I was not alone. Still higher climbed the waves, and the spray was now a giant whip as the mighty sailing ship lurched to one side and then the other.... Up went the bows and round went my intestines as a grey-green hue commenced to blotch my cheeks.

Suddenly, to my alarm, rope ladders were being pushed down over the sides of the vessel.... There was something ominous about the urgency of the cadets as they milled around the captain, who looked frozen with fear.... There was a lot of chattering in Polish, then, to my horror, lifejackets started to appear. I fought to get the first one....

Tracy, a glass of brandy in her hand, held on to a mast while she listened to me scream in panic, then she drained the glass and nonchalantly descended back down into the bar. She had no lifebelt on, but did I think of giving her mine? 'Don't worry,' I screeched to an elderly lady hanging on to the bowsprit and clutching a Gideon Bible, 'it's only some sort of training exercise for the cadets.' She glared at me and although I could never swear to it in a court of law, I thought I heard her shout: 'Exercise my backside, we're abandoning the bleedin' boat.'

Before I could laugh at her fears, I received another stream of cold salt water down my neck and went to pieces as I watched several trembling cadets winding down the lifeboats into the water.

Tracy reappeared, this time wearing a lifebelt, and I knelt at her feet and begged her to get me into the first lifeboat by telling the captain that I was her sister.

Battered and deafened by the angry wind, wet through, and robbed of gravity by a ship that was floundering about like an oversexed haddock, I tried to look carefree, and as the first lifeboat full of old women and a few kids dropped into the sea, I began to sing 'Abide With Me'. Nobody laughed, even when I tried to leap into the lifeboat with a bribe in my hand.

Finally Tracy and I were helped into the last lifeboat and she asked me to stop crying so openly.

As we bounced away from the sailing ship, it was most disconcerting to see a large jagged rent in the ship's timbers, just above the water line. Apparently the 'judder' we had felt as we left the harbour had been the noise of the stone groyne grinding into the side of the ship. The inexperienced captain had decided it was too dangerous to attempt a return to the harbour, and so we, the passengers, had been jettisoned and here we were, miles from land, tossing and pitching in frail craft.... Never again, I resolved, would I shake a fist to the gods....

It took hours to get back to Douglas and I had to be partly lifted up the stone harbour steps by muscular mariners. People crowded around and I was just about to hold court and tell of my bravery and how I saved the ship, when I caught Tracy's eye and thought better of it.

I was wet, fed up, cold and sick, but I felt a whole lot better when we all trooped into a pub.

Thus ended another momentous holiday break.

I'd started doing after-dinner speeches to try and glean a few bob. Television had deserted me and the theatres and cabaret dates had dried up, and if you didn't walk on a stage and open your act by shouting 'F... off', well, you were not considered a comedian. I was finding things difficult and what was worse, I was losing confidence in myself.

So it was that I started doing after-dinner speaking.

> *'In 1645 Prince Rupert's mercenaries smashed Cromwell's left flank at Naseby, and in 1871 the Franco-Prussian War took a serious turn at Metz, and in 1906 from the Kyles of Bute came the first report of an outbreak of sporran rash .... None of this has anything to do with tonight's event, but it just shows how your mind wanders when you're worried.'*

That was the opening line of my after-dinner speech and it certainly got the attention of some difficult audiences.

Looking back now, I still get flabbergasted at the amount of running about Tracy and I managed to do that year. Robson Books published my new book, *Well Fared, My Lovely* which was a send-up of every gangster novel ever written. The opening chapter gives you some idea of what the plot was all about:

> 'I was sat in my office, the curtains were drawn but the rest of the furniture was real. Suddenly my ears began to ring and when I answered them it was a wrong number. Just then

> a letter was pushed under the door, and it brought tears to my eyes ... it was written on an onion. I thought, Aye, aye, that's shallot.... Why should I worry, I get a good celery. Fifi swaggered into the office and started licking my cheek. "I don't love you pal – I need the salt," she said.'

Totally barmy, but there was a lot of interest in it, so off we trooped to publicise it.

First stop on our tour was at the headquarters of W H Smith near Oxford. They were doing a big promotion on my book and I spoke to their sales staff ... 'Great pleasure to be here on behalf of Smith's – which is Menzies with a sneer.' 'Wonderful lunch, I couldn't fault it – wasn't enough to form an opinion.' Yes, I know all the old gags but they were well received.

In quick succession I appeared on *Pebble Mill, Wogan, TV AM, The Gloria Hunniford Show,* plus radio shots with Mike Parkinson and Michael Aspel. We were driving around the country like maniacs and in between I had to sandwich conference dates where I performed and handed out prizes, a visit to Wales to open a giant supermarket, and a press call in Wimbledon for the pantomime there that season.

Tiredness and fatigue were our constant companions and Tracy was getting depressed about the incessant treadmill of work and travel. Whenever possible, we drove home, always in the early hours of the morning, but there was never enough time to relax, and it was beginning to show, especially on me. I was smoking and drinking far too much. All my weight was back, hanging in sinister folds, and I was a bloodshot-eyed mess. We'd been married over two years and Tracy had had little or no home life, nor had a decent holiday. All we'd managed to get in was a four-day break in Paris for our wedding anniversary. Ah! Paris in May.... Young lovers lost in each other's arms ... the smell of coffee and tobacco... the raucous symphony of the traffic round the Place de la Concorde ... night settling on the twinkling city with a scented caress as the Seine carries the glittering boats past Notre Dame. That's how it should have been. The reality was that it was the coldest May Paris had ever known.

Bone-chilling winds curved up into Montmartre and created a terrible draught in Les Halles, but after a while the raging winds became tempered by the lashing rain that swept across the Left Bank and turned it into a monsoon ditch.

Tracy and I were the only ones sitting outside the Café de la Paix on the corner of the Opera House – and all the other customers were tied to tables inside in case the storm blew them away. As we sipped our coffee and iced rain, first wiping the frost from our lips, Tracy's spirit broke. She turned her blue face to me and said: 'This is bloody stupid, never ask me to come away with you again – you are a flaming jinx.'

We saw the shows and sailed down the Seine on our actual anniversary date; the weather held its breath in a respite from the elements, and the waxy moon threw back the quilt of dusk and probed our little vessel as we toasted our love in champagne, which cost nearly as much as the boat.

Looking back to that May, I've often pondered on the possibility of suing God.

We had to walk along the city streets in a hunched posture hoping to stop the blustery wind from spinning us into windmills, that physical position also helped to allow the rain to cascade into a sort of funnel down our backs, which after drowning one's trousers gurgled happily down the drains.

The final indignity came the day we were thawing out in the hotel bedroom. As Tracy's teeth chattered I gave up trying to force broth down her cramped throat, so instead I wrapped her up in the blankets and sent her down for a bucket of hot coals. I turned the television set on and a panoramic view of a beach shivered into focus on the screen ... and what a view it was! Golden sand dunes baking under a torrid sun, graceful sand yachts speeding along a glittering seascape where timid wavelets ran ashore then swirled into retreat.... 'That's where we should be, Poo,' I said over my shoulder. I lit a cigarette, which was so damp it not only failed to ignite, but turned into a mess of bits that clung to my front teeth. Almost in tears I watched the sand yachts tack and veer, then I looked again. 'Jesus Christ,' I blasphemed. 'Poo, come and look at this.'

The pile of blankets jerked. 'What's the matter?' she whispered, her voice beginning to crack with flu.

'Look at the telly,' I screamed. 'Sand yachting.... Look.... It's bloody Lytham St Annes.'

It was true. The beach and the sea and the sand yachts belonged to the place we'd left two days ago... our home.

The flight home was uneventful for a change and as soon as we both shrugged off our mildewed clothes, we jumped into a hot bath and swallowed anti-pleurisy tablets, so ended another unforgettable sojourn, but it gave me some material....

'What a flight! the plane was an early jet, a bag of charcoal and an oven.'

'I said to the pilot "Do these planes crash often?" He said "No, only once...."'

'The weather was so bad in Paris they had lifeboat drill on the buses.'

Back home once more, there was no time to relax, it was off to the Midlands where I had an after-dinner speech to make, then on to London for another hotel conference. It was well into the early hours when we got to bed.

I wasn't sleeping well. Apart from troubled dreams, my chest was tight and I spent half the night hawking up mucus. I took pills and antibiotics but the chest condition didn't get any better, and Tracy's blue eyes were clouded with anxiety. But me? I was immortal, wasn't I? Twice I had cheated death, so they told me, that must mean I'm going to go on for ever, hey?

Quo Vadis, Clown?

The audience laughed at the little comic's jokes and shook their heads in disbelief at the outrageous faces he pulled.

'I took the wife out the other night. . . . I take her everywhere with me, it saves kissing her goodbye.'

'I had a nightmare last night, that the wife's mother was chasing me with a crocodile on a lead. . . . It was awful. I could feel the hot rancid breath on my neck. . . . I could hear the snap of the giant teeth and the murderous look in the dirty yellow eyes. . . . If you think that was bad enough, wait till I tell you about the crocodile.'

'I've always kept a photograph of the mother-in-law on the mantelpiece . . . it keeps the kids away from the fire.'

'The wife's mother's been married three times. Her first two died through eating poisoned mushrooms, the third one died with an arrow in his back. I said to her: "How terrible! How come he was killed by an arrow?" She said, "Because he wouldn't eat the bloody mushrooms."'

What the audience didn't see was the comic's body rebelling against all the abuse it had sustained; and what he didn't know was that there would have to be a day of reckoning.

Tracy and I went on a book signing tour which was fun. . . . I enjoyed sitting behind a pile of books chatting and signing them, but fatigue was now getting to be a menace; it was as if we couldn't stop our helter-skelter pace of life, and on top of everything else, Tracy told me she wanted to start a family!

Naturally, I told her, I would like a baby, but I didn't tell her that I was worried about my ability to father one. After the book tour we went to a specialist for a mutual check-up. After all, Tracy was over forty, she'd had three miscarriages, and I didn't intend risking her life simply to have another child – we already had five between us. But every time she saw a baby her eyes would soften, and well . . . what can a man do?

Tracy was given the all-clear with her health, and the specialist turned his attention to me. . . . He went on at length about giving a sample of semen and I tried to wriggle out of that one. Many many years ago, I had been deeply embarrassed in a Manchester hospital trying to do a sample in a bottle whilst sitting on a lavatory seat with my right foot jammed against the door because there was no lock on it. If that wasn't bad enough, a man waiting increasingly impatiently to get in the loo finally shouted through the door: 'What the bleedin' hell are you doing in there, mate – having a wank?' He could never know how true the gibe was. Now I was being asked to do it again.

I looked at Tracy and in her eyes I saw her willing me to do it. I was frightened that I would not prove man enough to father a baby; after all, I was over fifty years of age; I had a weight problem; I'd had a mild heart attack; I no longer had a prostate gland, which meant that my flow of semen probably wouldn't be strong enough to fertilise the egg; I was a heavy drinker and smoked like a kipper-curing shed. A nice young man in a spotless white coat led me through a labyrinth of sterile corridors and eventually closeted me in a room with a bottle, a towel and stuff in a phial to wash my thingumajig with. In the spartan room was a trundle bed, painted grey, a hard upright chair, a shelf, and two brightly covered books depicting sexual positions that only a trained gymnast could get into.

'Er, these books,' said the Nice Young Man in the Spotless Coat, 'just in case you need them ... well, you know ... let me know when you've finished.'

With that parting shot he almost ran out of the room. I was alone. Have you ever tried to think about sex in the early afternoon in a hospital room with a sinister-looking bottle? I partly undressed and sat gingerly on the edge of the bed. I looked closely at the naked ladies in the book. They were about as erotic as a flock of homing pigeons, and one huge lady with a mat of pubic hair that grew up to her chin looked as if she'd be more at home in a Sumo training camp than lying on a mattress. I got into a position and started to masturbate, but my foot got hooked between the bars of the bed head and I fell off and cannoned into the radiator. I hoisted myself up on to the bed once more and tried to imagine I was about to make love to every film actress in the world, but the only image that kept recurring was that of Donald Duck – and that's the truth! Perhaps some psychiatrist will one day explain to me why I kept on thinking about Donald Duck, but I had to give the film actress idea up and look again at the National Health dirty book.

One position intrigued me. A rather thin gentleman with a quite outrageous penis was lying on the bed with one leg stuck up in the air and his other leg curled under his buttocks. The woman was lying on top of him with her head bobbing about somewhere round the gentleman's groin.... Purely in the interest of research I tried to imagine Tracy and myself in this position, and in doing so I developed severe cramp in the right calf muscle which caused me to bellow aloud with agony. The door burst open at the very moment my body decided to roll off the bed again – a young nurse took one look and ran off emitting shrieks of horror. As I clambered to my feet, my left shoe got trapped in my braces and twanged me into the wall just as the Nice Young Man in the Spotless White Coat entered the room to tell me that he'd explained to the horrified nurse that I wasn't a pervert or a lunatic, and therefore there was no need to send for the police. Already I'd been in the room for well over an hour, and the bottle remained empty.

I lit a fag and looked out of the window at the passing parade of hospital life, but there was no inspiration from that direction. I sent out for a cup of tea. That didn't help, and I started to get an attack of the giggles by imagining Donald Duck in black knickers and a garter belt.

Two hours gone, and still nothing to show for the tortuous positions, nothing to show for the mental sex orgies, and my heaving, sweating bulk, with tendrils of clothing still adhering to it, ached in every cramped sinew. Once or twice somebody knocked but went away hurriedly as my coarse breathing rose in a series of wild pig grunts and snorts.... I was losing my marbles. Finally, I stood naked on top of the bed and gave vent to a loud animal cry.... There was a blob of semen in the bottle. Swiftly I parcelled the bottle in layers of tissue, determined that no living soul should see the result of my infamy.

I rang a bell and a large triangular nurse opened the door, took the bottle off me, unwrapped it and boomed down the corridor: 'SO YOU'VE FINALLY MANAGED A SAMPLE, HAVE YOU? ABOUT TIME.'

If I'd had a scalpel I would have plunged it deep

between her shoulder blades, then turned it on myself.

Tracy looked tired after her prolonged wait, and remarked that I looked a trifle peculiar.

I was summoned into another room, a small laboratory, where an earnest young boffin gazed at me owlishly. I felt certain he was going to tell me that my sperms had long since passed away with age and alcohol. Instead, his face creased into one huge smile and he said: 'Wonderful result, Mr Dawson, your sperm count is one of the highest I've ever seen. Congratulations!' I walked out of that hospital on a cushion of air. I was for the moment, a king.

As soon as we arrived home, I poured out a glass of champagne each, we drank, and then I put forward the motion that an early night was indicated.... Tracy readily agreed.

The year was speeding into early autumn ... just where does time go? There were one or two engagements to fulfil; the first was an invitation to speak at a Variety Club Charity Luncheon that was being held in honour of Frankie Howerd at the Hilton Hotel on Park Lane. Cilla Black was one of the other speakers at the celebrity-studded occasion and the veteran comedian was flushed with the accolades heaped on him. I was proud to speak because I had always admired him ... a unique humorist, sadly missed.

The other big event was to be the after-dinner speaker at a Co-operative function at the Tara Hotel in Kensington. I enjoyed that date mainly because of nostalgia, I suppose. When I left school at fourteen my mother had urged me to 'get a job with security and a pension'. With hindsight, it's an appalling thought that a fourteen-year-old boy should be choosing an occupation for the pension, but my parents, who'd never known security, looked upon a job like that as manna from heaven, and so after two interviews I gained employment as a junior drapery warehouse operative. The job entailed pulling large skips of merchandise from one big sorting warehouse into another one where people stood and packaged the goods for shipment. It was the most boring job a youngster could have, running half crouched and crabwise, backwards and forwards, all day long, and all for the princely wage of twenty-two shillings and ninepence.... But it had a pension!

Tracy and I spent a lot of time in our London flat in Buckingham Gate, round the corner from the Palace. Our favourite pastime was walking through St James's Park, mixing with the characters and feeding the ducks. Sounds nothing, doesn't it? But with the hectic life we were living, this simple pleasure was divine for us, and our companionship was complete; no false friends, no favours to be demanded ... just a man and his wife and the park.

Often, as we strolled round the park, I would see Tracy look longingly at proud young mothers pushing prams containing loved little ones, and I knew how passionately she wanted a child of our own.

I was concerned about my future in show business. There was the panto coming up in Wimbledon, but my television career looked to be on the rocks, and having lived through bad times I didn't relish the idea of going through them again, especially with a baby on board. But, just look at the longing in my wife's eyes....

The following week we managed to go back North to the home we adored but seldom saw. For a few days we became domestic recluses, and all else was put to one side. Although being at home was a time for peace and serenity, I still had hoped that somebody from a television company would phone and offer me something, but no offers came. I'd heard nothing from the BBC after the *Fast Friends* débâcle, and Yorkshire Television had dropped an idea they had for me, so the future was looking bleak.

After years at the top of my profession, I now felt unwanted and old, as if somebody had pressed an abort button on my life. Never having saved much money, financially I was far from secure, and for my sanity I simply had to work, but there was nothing in the conduit whatsoever. The world recession was biting, as everybody who went under will tell you, and work was hard to find.

I read one morning that the Queen had stated privately that in her considered opinion the annual Royal Variety Show was far too long, and if steps were not taken to tighten it up and shorten it, she would not grace it with her presence. Without her, the show would be quite unthinkable.

I had performed in ten royal shows, and every one was a nerve-racking experience. I'd appeared alongside such stars as Yul Brynner, Rosemary Clooney, Red Buttons, Bill Haley, Tony Bennett, James Mason, Dolores Grey, Jerry Lewis and hosts of other big names . . . and no matter how big, they all had knots in their stomachs.

Tracy and I went back to London to do a show for the BBC, *Children In Need*, a fine programme that raises a lot of money for all deprived and handicapped kids. My youngest daughter danced with Bruce Forsyth and I danced with his television hostess, Rosemary Ford . . . it was a good spot and a lot of laughs.

Whilst in London, my agents told me that London Weekend Television wanted me to appear on the Royal Show. I said thanks but no thanks – it was too nerve-racking. Norman informed LWT of my decision and that,

I thought, was that. It wasn't a question of being 'big time' or anything like that; I turned it down because it can break a comedian's career if he doesn't go down well, and I didn't have the confidence to face another setback when my career was already hanging by a thread – or so it seemed to me.

Again and again I was urged to change my mind but I refused. Then one day I received a phone call from a reporter on a London newspaper. 'How does it feel to be a royal favourite?' he asked. 'What the hell are you talking about?' I responded. There was a short pause, then he said, 'I thought you might have heard, when the list of acts was presented for approval, Prince Philip asked especially for you. Apparently you are well favoured by the Queen and Prince Philip.' I gulped and put the phone down. I found out later that the reporter was telling the truth, and so I readily agreed to be on the bill. What else could I do? If I was a falling star then I'd go out before my Queen. The die was cast.

London Weekend had gathered an awesome bill together. Top of the bill was singer Diana Ross, together with the great American humorist Jackie Mason. He was good, I'd seen him work. Ned Sherrin, David Frost, Elaine Paige, the entire cast of *Les Misérables*, up and coming funnymen Billy Pierce and Mike Doyle, Eric Idle, Wayne Sleep ... so many big names! It got to the stage where I was the only one I'd never heard of.

As the long days' rehearsals dragged on, I sat hunched in my seat in the darkened auditorium of the Victoria Palace. I watched all the performers go through their paces and their confidence and stage presence made me feel more and more inadequate. The younger comics seemed much more 'with it' both in style and material. Their jokes were simple and easy to understand, whilst my approach to comedy was a long-winded series of word pictures. Over and over again I mentally went through my script, and each time I did so it got less funny. There was a pub across the road from the theatre and it was open all day – and I used it all day.

Tracy kept reassuring me that everything would be fine, but her concern only served to increase my melancholy. . . . I felt doomed. On these occasions, the tension in a dressing-room is sometimes quite unbearable but Eric Idle and Ned Sherrin were witty companions. Soon the day became the BIG NIGHT. . . .

Tracy had to get me ready – for two pins I would have leapt on to the stage waving a white flag. My confidence was at rock bottom and I kept making alterations to the script: as far as I was concerned, it was about as comical as a dung beetle on a lump of ox shit.

The show opened with David Frost, who made the audience roar with some clever patter before introducing the cast from the hit musical *Buddy*. They brought the house down and I was feeling so low I could have crawled under a pancake and never caused a bump.

Young Billy Pierce was excellent, and so was Mike Doyle, who turned out not only to be a comedian but the possessor of a fine tenor voice . . . Christ! Where did they get so much talent?

Pop star Beverley Craven was a hit, and she made way for Ann Howard, the opera singer, and as if rendering 'One Fine Day' in a magnificent voice wasn't enough to sandbag any courage left in me, Eric Idle popped up and turned the whole thing into one huge exercise in laughter. . . . David Frost went on again to introduce some youngsters from an East European state and they played balalaikas like seasoned veterans. It was my turn to walk on to the stage and all my failures flashed before me . . .

my career, or what now passed for it, was in the hands of fate. Would the audience remember my triumphs, or would they just remember the many flops?

The lights hit me as I tried to saunter nonchalantly towards the centre stage area. Her Majesty had a smile on her face and Prince Philip looked as if he was hoping for a good laugh. I only hoped that I wouldn't disappoint them.

The audience settled, but there were one or two titters as I loomed before them, and they bolstered my ego somewhat. There was no going over the script again, no chance of deleting a gag and putting a stronger one in.... I was committed to what I'd memorised and that was that. I cleared my throat and began the act. Within a few minutes I would know whether I had anything of value to offer the public any more, and whether I still had a place in the world of entertainment.

'Good evening, the theatre management have asked me to inform you that they've lost the theatre cat, so if you see it will you please tell one of the usherettes? It's a nice cat, I always thought it had one eye then I realised it was walking backwards.'

'It's wonderful to be appearing here in this marvellous old theatre, such an intimate atmosphere ... it reminds me of home – it's filthy and full of strangers.'

'I've never forgotten the last time I appeared on the Royal Variety Show ... it was a triumph, a tour de force ... a night to remember. Her Majesty the Queen sat in the royal box and she wore a radiant smile on her face throughout my act ... and Prince Albert fell about.'

'Actually I shouldn't have been here at all tonight, I should have been on tour in a revival of the hit musical The King and I *with Madonna, but they had to cancel it. She wouldn't have her head shaved.'*

'Anyway, don't worry, I shall not keep you long, I promise. I do believe that one or two of you fancy an early night.' (The Queen loved that one!)

'It's been a disappointing year for many people. As we all know, this great nation of ours is going through a severe economic depression, not that the depression bothers me ... I was a failure during the boom.'

'I hear that they're building a new toilet in the House of Commons. I think it will be money well spent, because it's the only place where they know what they're doing.'

'No point in telling politicians to go to hell because they're building it for us.'

'I hear we may soon have a single Euro currency, what a great idea! ... Then we can go bankrupt in seven different languages.'

My act went a storm. The whole theatre rocked with laughter and Her Majesty laughed along with her subjects.... I overran by eight minutes, but nobody cared.... I was a sensation, and my confidence positively roared back. All the other performers crowded round me as I lit a cigarette with a shaking hand before leaving the theatre to go across the road to the pub to see Tracy and hear her verdict. It was my night.

Tracy rushed through the smoky, crowded bar and threw herself into my arms. 'Oh Les,' she breathed happily, 'you were great ... I'm so proud of you ... and I love you so much.'

I'd finished my act with a bit at the piano and I'd been joined by Mo and the Roly Polys. They now came into the pub to cheers from the habitués. We ordered a plenitude of drinks and watched the remainder of the show on the television screen that had been erected in the pub ... but I couldn't come down from cloud nine. I was so thrilled that I'd done so well; I felt that I had vindicated myself after my apparent dismissal by the television companies.

We lined up after the finale in readiness to meet Her Majesty and Prince Philip, and I knew by her face as we shook hands that she'd really enjoyed it. Prince Philip grinned at me with his customary salutation: 'Hello, Dawson.' Cherished memories.

Tracy and I attended a big post-show party at producer Paul Elliot's house and it was very, very late when our driver got us home from London. We tumbled into bed utterly exhausted – but we couldn't stay in bed on the morrow, no sirree, because old workaholic Dawson had to drag himself and Tracy to Manchester Airport in order to catch a flight to Edinburgh ... and from there to be driven fifty-odd miles to Gleneagles, where I was booked to do a cabaret spot. Tracy was not amused.

The newspapers were full of glowing reviews of the Royal Show, and I was described as the 'show stealer'. I read them all on the flight to Scotland.

The Gleneagles is a superb hotel and I love its grandeur and stylish good taste. The cabaret spot went very well; the weather, however, was turning decidedly chilly and the forecast said it was worsening. I could see that there'd be no chance of a game of golf, so we decided to curtail our stay and fly back to Manchester.

When we arrived at Edinburgh Airport the weather was atrocious: sheets of hailstones lashing across the runway and no sign of a break in the thick black mantle of cloud. There weren't a lot of passengers for our flight – thankfully, as it turned out.

We fastened our seat belts and I snuggled down, hoping to grab a few precious minutes of sleep.... 'I can smell something burning,' said Tracy loudly, compensating for the noise of the thrust of the engines as we started to take off. 'I can't smell anything, love,' I rejoined and pulled my battered straw hat back over my eyes. Suddenly I heard the engines die down and the young stewardess shouting in a strained tone: 'Please leave the aircraft as quickly as possible. Leave your luggage behind – please hurry.' I looked out of the cabin porthole and saw fire tenders and men in bulky suits ringing the aeroplane as snow flurries danced and wheeled in the grip of an incensed wind. The aircraft was on fire! A few seconds later and we would have been in the air.... God knows what would have happened then.

With only a thin jacket on, I was soon soaked to the skin as we waited for transport to take us back to the terminus. Several of the female passengers were hysterical and one had to be tranquillised. I looked at Tracy and she looked at me, and we stalked arm in arm to the airport bar and did some dedicated drinking.... We'd had a narrow escape – why we were spared, I don't know, but all the way home on another flight I smelt freesias.

The following day I scanned most of the newspapers but there was no mention of the incident at Edinburgh Airport.

I now had another small battle on my hands. I received a letter from the main Post Office in Blackpool saying how sorry they were that I'd had recourse to the press to complain that I'd had trouble with my postal delivery. 'Here we go again,' I thought and immediately phoned the chap who'd written to me. I told him that I had not complained about my postal delivery to anyone, let alone a newspaper. I thought that would scotch the silly story but the morning after several national newspapers carried a small mention of the story, and in the afternoon the supervisor called at my home with the postal cadet who delivers my letters. He had apparently been asked by one newspaper to see if I would have a photograph taken with the cadet. I refused, because to have done so would indicate that I had said something about the Post Office in the first place – it is banal stories such as this, based on no foundation whatsoever, that can create a lot of trouble. In one paper, for instance, it stated: 'Dawson who earns a fortune off the Post Office commercial blasts his postman'. I wish it had been a fortune, mate, then I could have had Christmas off and devoted more time to writing my books.

Tracy and I enjoyed our brief time at home together, planting things in the garden, messing about with our two dogs, Samson, a rather peculiar poodle, and Delilah, a very large St Bernard. One also has to make a great fuss of the cats, Muffin and Merlin, not to mention the rabbits, Thumper and Patch. Life without animals is unthinkable for Tracy, and despite my protests I've now become a sort of Doctor Doolittle.

We took to going for long walks on the magnificent sands of St Annes, with Tracy striding out vigorously, the sea breezes ruffling her hair into lengthy knots, while I grovelled in the damp sand in the rear, with aching lungs, a St Bernard lovingly trying to stand on top of me, and a poodle joyously licking my face and hands. Simple pleasures to be sure, but to us it was wonderful.

All too soon work beckoned in the shape of pantomime in Wimbledon. I'd never played the theatre there but when Tracy and I went down for the press call I was very impressed with it. It had been beautifully and lovingly restored, and the management couldn't do enough for us.

The cast was as usual a strong one. I was to play Ada

the cook, with John Nettles as King Rat, Rula Lenska as Dick Whittington, and young comic Jeff Stevenson as Idle Jack – and not forgetting the Roly Polys as the ship's crew!

During the rehearsals I accepted interviews with press and radio. I joked on television and still found time to go out and plug my book. The advance bookings were excellent and all augured well for a successful run of seven weeks, then on to the Grand Theatre, Leeds, for a further two-week run. Nothing could go wrong this time, could it? There was a secret excitement when it was learned that Mighty Mo, my dear friend from the Roly Polys, was to be the subject of *This Is Your Life*. I was to greet Michael Aspel at the stage door and bring him into the theatre, where he would hide until the end of the show. Trying to keep a secret from Mo was worse than trying to get Cyril Smith to go on the 'F-plan' diet. Somehow we all managed to keep it dark – and then on the night Mo decided to plonk herself down in my dressing-room at the same time as I was supposed to go down and let Michael Aspel in. To do the interview outside the stage door meant rigging up lighting and sound equipment, and as my dressing-room was immediately above the stage door, Mo would see and hear everything and smell a rat. So Tracy and I had to be deliberately rude to her, walking out of the dressing-room, saying as we went that we had something important to discuss. Poor Mo looked so hurt that I damn nearly told her! However, the ploy worked and a very disgruntled Mo left the dressing-room wondering what on earth she'd done.

I had one last trick to play on her. So that Aspel could get on the stage and come forward to challenge Mo with his famous red book, I had to bring her to the edge of the stage away from the other Roly Polys, so that the concealed cameras could catch the moment. I told a big lie; I said that there was a party of women out front in the audience and they were all fans of the Roly Polys and could Mo step forward at the end of the show and wave to them? As it turned out, the whole thing worked wonderfully well and as Mike Aspel showed her the book saying as he did so: 'Mo Moreland, this is your life', she hugged me and said, 'So that's why you and Tracy were funny with me!'

It was six thirty in the morning when Tracy and I got back to our flat.... I have never felt so tired. I was drunk, and every limb ached ... instinctively I knew I was heading for trouble, though I didn't realise how soon that was to be.

The critics raved at the opening of *Dick Whittington*, and Mo's *This Is Your Life* was an added spice to the night. I virtually had to drag myself to the theatre for the matinée, and my tiredness had tightened every nerve in my body to breaking point. The last time I'd felt so tense was the night we arrived in Belfast for a television show. We had been in the hotel only half an hour when a car bomb exploded outside the hotel entrance. The explosion sent a sucking vacuum of hot air up the side of the building and the whole hotel shuddered and rocked. For the rest of the night I was a very uneasy little comedian and I was glad to see Blackpool Airport again – I'm no politician and the whys and wherefores of dogma elude me – but does violence solve anything?

Anyway, on that fateful Saturday at the Wimbledon Theatre, I somehow got through the matinée, then Tracy tried to get me to have forty winks between houses, but I was too tired to sleep and my chest was bubbling with mucus to the extent that I found breathing difficult. I dashed down a large gin and lit up yet another cigarette, much to Tracy's anger and disgust. She was concerned, I knew, but I thought a good night's sleep would put me back on form.

As soon as the curtain dropped on the evening's performance, Tracy bundled me into the waiting hire car and we sped off to our flat. I didn't feel too bad at that stage, just dog tired and bloated. Tracy made some supper and I watched a little television. She went off to bed leaving me watching a trite Western. I lit a cigarette and lay prone on the carpet intent on seeing the showdown between the gunslinger and the Man From Laramie.... I was destined never to see if justice prevailed, because at that moment I found that I couldn't breathe ... my intake of air was lessening with each inhalation. I scrambled to my feet and my head swam, I fell to a kneeling position.... No air was going into my lungs, I could neither breathe in nor out fully and I sensed that I was going to die. Tracy shouted to me from the bedroom and I tried to shout back, but I was totally unable to do so. I was labouring for every little breath. Finally, as I felt myself slipping away, I croaked, 'Tracy ... get a doctor.' The dear girl came running into the lounge and her face went the colour of chalk.

How she did it I do not know, but within a minute or two she had got hold of a doctor – who was trying to find a vein to pump something into me – and two paramedics, who turned the room into a bloodbath whilst attempting to help the doctor find the elusive vein. This was an almost impossible task because my blood pressure was dangerously low and my heart was overtaxed. Eventually one of the paramedics found a tiny pulse in my neck and gave me an injection; it didn't help me to breathe but it relaxed me a little and it gave them a chance to carry me into the lift then get me into the ambulance. I lay on the stretcher with an oxygen mask on and Tracy at my side in tears. Fighting for air I watched the city lights streak by and the siren on the ambulance seemed to scream at me: 'You bloody fool ... you were given another chance, and what have you done? You've abused it.' I dimly recall them saying to Tracy at the Westminster Hospital as they rushed me into the intensive care cardiac unit, 'Mrs Dawson, prepare yourself, Les might not make it.'

A team of quiet efficient people worked over me ... GIVE ME AIR ... PLEASE. Everything was growing darker ... so tired ... Tracy's face is streaked with tears.... 'Don't cry, Poo, I'm gonna make it....'

The darkened room began to swim and I was being pulled into a black hole ... was this death?

I woke up in the early morning and a nurse rushed forward and made me swallow some pills, then blow into an air meter and sniff some stuff ... God ... I was alive! And Tracy was smiling and she was saying over and over, 'I love you, Lumpy.' I jerked upright and held her close. 'I love you, darling,' I whispered. 'I owe you my life and you are my life.'

My agent Norman arrived, panic-stricken that his meal ticket was slipping away and that he might have to go back to work. There I was lying in bed, every part of me including my private parts wired to some contraption or other and looking as if I was auditioning for *Alien 3*. Norman stopped at the foot of my bed, his eyes moist with pure disbelief and said, 'I've heard of not wanting to play the matinée, but this is ridiculous.'

Although I felt immeasurably better on the Sunday, nevertheless the nurses made it abundantly clear that I had been very ill indeed. My lungs had been almost full of fluid, and that had in turn put heavy pressure on my heart and I had nearly died. It was Tracy's swift action that had saved me from the Grim Reaper.

A consultant marched into the intensive care unit in the afternoon, and judging by the apprehension shown by the doctors who swarmed round her, she was a redoubtable woman. By God, she was. She looked down on me with a steely glare that matched her steely silver hair, and her firm chin and hard mouth decided me not to try and crack any jokes. Quietly but tellingly she stated that fortunately I had not suffered a heart attack but I had damaged my heart. The gist of the conversation was: I was a bloody fool, overdoing it to a silly extent; it was essential that I stopped smoking at once – or else! – and, perhaps worst of all, no more spirits and a general lessening of wine and beer intake.

Plenty of sleep was also advocated and no, I couldn't go back into the pantomime, and she told my agents this in no uncertain manner. No, I couldn't go home, I was being kept in for tests, and no, I couldn't get out of bed, and no, I couldn't have food brought in. I didn't argue because I sensed that I'd be a loser with this formidable lady.

Tracy stayed in hospital with me and saved my sanity. Opposite my bed lay a gentleman who had suffered a major heart attack, and to see him there so pitifully ill made me very sad. Beside me in the ward was a successful business executive who had driven to his place of work, had a cup of coffee, dictated some letters to his secretary, then slumped to the floor behind his desk with a massive coronary. What price success now?

As expected, the newspapers carried the story of my collapse and every account differed from the others. In one lurid headline I had crumpled up on the stage and been dragged off to make way for the dancers; in another account I had fallen into the orchestra pit and impaled myself on an oboe. Television news told of my plight as did the radio stations ... what a way to get publicity!

I began not only to fully respect the consultant, but to like her as well ... she was as straight a person as I've ever met and I obeyed her every dictum. She brought me down to earth by simply refusing even to smile at my jokes, although the nurses, bless 'em, giggled.

Christmas Eve in hospital ... what, I thought, could be worse? I had helped Tracy and the nurses to put the Christmas decorations up and the splash of colour softened the green-grey walls. Tracy and I held hands and occasionally kissed which was difficult with all the bits and pieces hanging out of me, but we managed. Suddenly the silence in the hospital was broken by the sound of Christmas carols being sung down the corridors – a sweet sound from young hearts reminding us of the timeless message of love. The nurses walked into our ward like angels, their red capes atop their prim uniforms, each carrying aloft a lantern. They sang the familiar carols which somehow sounded even more moving in the presence of mortals who had fought off death. Tracy's hand gripped mine as we watched and listened. No cathedral could have provided a better setting for that group standing in the broad halo of light from their lanterns.

There was so much love in their singing, it spread a canopy of peace over the sick in every ward and room that the nurses went into. In a strange way, I was glad that we were there that Christmas Eve to share the experience.

On Christmas Day we helped set a long trestle table down the centre of the ward, and staff and patients alike sat down to enjoy a turkey dinner and pull a few crackers. When my agent came in even that hard-bitten old devil was visibly moved to see the patients – drips and tubes and all – toasting each other, the doctors and nurses, friends and loved ones, in the glass of wine we were allowed with the festivities.

I was once again moved by the masses of flowers and all the goodwill cards sent to me, proving surely that I wasn't forgotten. I realised just how much I had to live for, and I vowed that from now on, I would cut out of my existence the sham of ambition.

Three days later I was discharged. The Iron Maiden came to see me before I left the hospital, and as usual the staff trembled when she appeared. I did, however, have a weapon that I hoped would find a chink in her armour: someone had told me her first name! A lovely, wholly feminine, moniker. 'Don't forget: no smoking! No drinking! No late nights! You have been very ill in large measure due to your stupidity.' She was wonderful, there should be more like her – and believe me, I listened. We shook hands with her and as she reached the door I piped up: 'Thanks for everything, I shall never forget you ... dear Lavinia.'

She stiffened like a ramrod, but then I saw her shoulders shake with laughter! To all the staff at Westminster Hospital, my gratitude for the care and the courtesy, and to those two paramedics who fought for me that dark night – many thanks, fellows. And to Tracy, my wife ... words are simply inadequate. It was good to get home.

After a New Year's Eve celebration at my agent's house in Highgate, Tracy and I drove home to our beloved Lancashire, and that little piece of paradise: Garth House, Lytham.

The yawning sandy beaches of St Annes on Sea, the

wide roads and clean air, the lovely vulgar mistress that is Blackpool, always beckoning with a saucy finger to the thrills she can offer.... Home at last.

A Promise of a Little Sunshine

'An elderly couple, both in their late nineties, filed for a divorce. The solicitor couldn't believe it! He asked the husband: "You've been married for over fifty years, and now you say you want a divorce ... why?" The husband replied: "I never loved the old bag." His wife glared at him and said: "I must have been out of my mind when I said 'Yes' to that silly old sod. I can't stand him." The solicitor shook his head and said in a voice of wonder: "You've never liked one another yet you've had five children. If you hated each other that much why on earth didn't you get divorced years ago?" The old lady said: "We both agreed to wait until the kids died."'

'I made a big difference to my parents' lives, because before I was born my father had a nasty habit of running off and leaving my mother for months on end; then, when I came on the scene, they both gazed at me in the crib, held hands – then ran off together.'

'Although we were poor, my dad used to say to me: "One day, son, I'll have enough money to take you to Venice, and we'll ride up and down all day on the Grand Canal in a Gorgonzola." I said: "But Daddy, dear, that's a lump of cheese." He replied: "Who the hell cares as long as it doesn't leak?"'

The little comedian was heartened by the laughter, but Fate was planning a surprise that would send all his anxieties running for cover.... The Gods had decided to give him a smile....

* * *

The first step for me, under Tracy's stern gaze, was to quit smoking ... and every smoker will tell you what a task that is. One method of stopping smoking is to stand naked in a draught in order to catch a cold, which might turn to rheumatic fever and also give you such a sore throat it will be agony to drag on a fag. That should put you off puffing for a few days at least until you start chewing a Fisherman's Friend and throw up. This is a good method and can be quite exciting if the woman next door decides to use it to stop smoking.

Now, let us assume that a week has gone by and you haven't touched a cigarette, and you hate everybody, and when friends visit you in a halo of gorgeous filter-tipped smoke, the first impulse is to club them to a grisly death with your noisiest offspring. To combat the smoking friends syndrome, drop each one of them a poison pen letter wrapped up in a section of lung, and keep them away by playing a Des O'Connor album.

Healthwise, despite what they say, you won't feel any improvement; in fact you may sustain concussion from banging your head against a wall when the craving gets too much to bear. Some well-meaning friends suggest hypnotism to help give up the habit. I went to see a certain Dr Hans Schemmingfester, formerly the head of a clinic for the chronically withered in Rhyl. Before the war he was a dressmaker in a Berlin flute orchestra and he once put a cow in labour to sleep. He was awarded the Iron Cross for opening an Arab dustbin in the heat of battle, and he was noted for having moved Rommel's bowels. He hypnotised me into thinking that every time I fancied a cigarette I would start to howl like a bull terrier.... It worked all right, in fact Tracy nearly divorced me after I had a brief affair with the St Bernard. Weight becomes the next problem because you are forever raiding the fridge. I became so fat, every time I stood on a 'Speak Your Weight' machine, it yelled, 'No coach parties!'

Anyway, I have now kicked the habit completely and I must admit that I can now climb a flight of stairs without begging for an oxygen mask. I gave up drinking whisky, which shocked show business and the distillers, and now I drink wine, in far smaller quantities, I might add.

Tracy also got me into the habit of going to bed early. The subject of starting a family cropped up again one night, and naturally I agreed to undergo rehearsals for it.... I was never ill enough to forgo that pleasure! However, there was another scare to face.

Tracy was busying herself in the kitchen one blustery late February morning, and I noticed that she was not her usual radiant self. When I taxed her about her health, she smiled, a little tensely I thought, and replied that she was fine. However, I became worried about her – her skin seemed to lack lustre and she was terribly tired all the time.... Despite her protests, I made an appointment for her to have some blood tests and a thorough general check-up. Five days later I drove her to see the specialist. I had already made provisional arrangements to take her away to where there might be some sunshine, because she looked so washed out, perhaps not surprisingly with all the anxiety over my illness, and the fast tempo of our lives. I blamed myself for her condition.

The blood tests were carried out efficiently, and the specialist, sensing my worry, told us to go and have a cup of coffee and come back in an hour for the results. I thanked him profusely, and off we went in a high old state of nervous tension to gulp down several cups of indifferent coffee.

'What do you think is wrong with me, Lump?' Tracy said quietly, but by the way she gripped her coffee cup I knew she was frightened. Normally she is as chirpy as a cricket, but now she was pale, very tired looking and dispirited.

'Don't worry, Poo,' I chortled falsely. 'You're probably a wee bit anaemic ... perhaps you need a tonic at your age.'

She smiled dutifully and whispered back, 'You are the only tonic I need.'

Tears sprang to my eyes.... I prayed to God that there was nothing seriously wrong with her. I couldn't live without her.... I'd lost before, please, not again, not now that I'd found another soulmate.

Back at the hospital I paced back and forth in the tiny office like a rampant polecat while Tracy bit her lip. The door opened and three nurses came in with long faces. One of them held a couple of tissues and I nearly screamed out: *'Christ, what's wrong with my wife?'* The solemn-faced nurse holding the Kleenex said: 'I thought you might need these ... Tracy, you're pregnant!'

I jumped up and started babbling with sheer joy, and Tracy's tiredness left her features and within seconds she was her old self! WE WERE GOING TO HAVE A BABY....

I kissed my wife, I kissed the beaming nurses ... I damn near kissed the walls of the tiny office. Never, since the miracle of the birth of my eldest child, now aged twenty-six, had I experienced such joy, such happiness! If ever a baby was wanted, if ever a child was conceived with love, it was that tiny seed in Tracy's womb.

As we drove home, so great was our happiness that we waved to surly motorists and tough-looking lorry drivers.... We thought of names for our baby. The doctor had told us there was nothing to worry about, tiredness was common in the early stages of pregnancy. Someone had heard my prayers, of that I'm convinced.

Although we decided to keep quiet about it, I wanted everyone we knew to share in our happiness, and – old blabbermouth me – I was soon on the phone to our closest friends. Mo, my original Roly Poly, was the first! Tracy and I flew up to Aberdeen to see her sister Marion and husband David, and had a wonderful four days. When we arrived home, there was a message on the answering machine from a newspaper reporter. Somehow they'd found out, but this time I couldn't have cared less if they'd heard about it in Borneo. I telephoned the paper and admitted we were going to have an addition to the family, and, yes, they could come round and take photographs, which they did, and every national newspaper carried the story of our baby-to-be.

It is surprising what news like that can do to people. The press were absolutely wonderful, one tabloid sent us a case of champagne, another a superb basket of flowers and fruit. Total strangers beamed at us in supermarkets or on the streets. And goodwill messages came in bushels. It was as if our love and the child Tracy was bearing were something we were meant to share with others ... and that we did gladly.

The thought of becoming a father again took twenty years off me. I was feeling on top of the world and a lot healthier since I'd stopped smoking and moderated my lifestyle. (Did I really once stay out all night in search of excitement?)

One more miracle to marvel at.... Tracy went to the hospital a few weeks later for a scan to ensure that everything was all right with the pregnancy, and there on a video screen, I saw the tiny being within her, a new life ... our child.

The Iron Maiden had informed my agents that on no

account was I to go back to work until the summer, and with so much to look forward to I complied with her dictum.

It wasn't easy; I felt out of things. The telephone didn't ring very much, there were no producers offering contracts, and I had to come to terms with my absence from the razzamatazz of show business. However, to stroll along the beach with Tracy, chatting about the coming birth, was a soothing balm to my ruffled feathers.

One or two things clouded my vista of happiness; the death of Frankie Howerd and the shock demise of Benny Hill . . . two funny men who gave pleasure to so many. I was saddened to hear that another fine performer, Roy Castle, had contracted cancer. I telephoned him with what must have sounded a strange message of hope. . . . 'Be angry' I said to Roy, and I meant it. As I wrote earlier, I believe in anger as a therapy. Rail against the powers that be for inflicting pain and suffering on you; rage at God if need be, He's big enough to know you don't really mean it!

I was due to play Bournemouth for a short summer season but would my health stand up to it? Only way to find out, buster – do it, and so I signed on for another run of the play *Run For Your Wife*.

Within myself, I felt a return of the confidence that ill health had taken away from me. Quite often when I mixed with other comedians, I'd felt insecure and unable to compete with them, now there was a spring in my step, I was ready to pick myself up, dust myself down and start all over again!

If I had one problem, well, it's one that is shared by many others: weight. Having stopped smoking I found that my sense of smell and taste had returned and my appetite had blossomed. What to do about it? It gave me an idea for a script.

Health Farm: The one I went to cost four hundred pounds, which was taken off you at the door by a shifty-looking Cypriot. What appealed to me about this health spa was that one could eat whatever one wanted, there was only one snag – they wouldn't let you swallow it.

The Celebrated Lancashire Seafood Diet: Very simple, all the food you see, you eat.

How To Be A Light Eater: Once again, simplicity itself – as soon as it's light – eat.

The French have a superb method for weight reduction: 7 lbs off immediately – la Guillotine.

I tried burning off the fat but it was costing a fortune in matches....

I tried to exist on vitamins B, C, D, E, and all that happened was I threw up alphabetically.

I finally found the solution and I gladly pass it on to you free of charge:

Find a backstreet tailor who can keep his mouth shut and order three suits (you should get a discount).
The first one should be a little tight fitting, the second one should be too big and the third one absolutely massive.
Put the first suit on and go to the doctor of your choice.
Straight away, whilst he's working out his golf handicap, he'll tell you to go on a strict diet.
Wait a month and then go back to his surgery in the second suit. The doctor will crow with admiration at the sight of you in the baggy suit. Weightwatchers will award you five points, and a highly trained team of specialists will examine your blood pressure and yell out that it's never been better.
Wait another month, then return to see the doc; this time garbed in the massive music hall suit.
When he sees you waddle into the surgery, he'll turn pale, grip you

tightly around the knees and beg you not to overdo it, in fact he will insist that you start drinking again to help build yourself up, together with eating lots of hot pies and chips.

Lastly, go home to roast beef and Yorkshire pud, put the first suit back on and everyone will tell you in the pub that you've never looked better.'

I was realising just how much I owed Tracy. Apart from tending to my needs and scolding me to look after myself more, she was a tower of strength in trying times. When Stuart, my son, crashed his racing car on the track at Castle Donington and the ambulance sped him away from the burning wreckage, it was she who calmed me down when I tried to leap the barrier.

Again, when we awakened from an exhausted doze by a frantic call from Julie, saying that Stuart (here we go again!) had crashed his racing car at Brands Hatch and was apparently at death's door, it was Tracy who prevented me from jumping off the gable end, Tracy who calmly phoned the hospital to get the true picture of his injuries, which by the mercy of God, were slight....

It was Tracy who laughed at a certain newspaper story purporting that I had sexually harassed make-up girls in the television studio! Strange really, because I was told the girls always asked to be on my show. It was a load of journalistic tripe, and the girls were the first to wax indignant over it, but a thing like that does tend to make you feel unclean, not to mention giving rise to the 'never smoke without fire' attitude in some. Not Tracy, she knew it was a falsehood and her trust in me will never be broken.

Despite worries about my future, it was nice to have time to have a social life. I was also finding that my capacity to hold vast volumes of alcohol had now shrunk with every passing day of teetotalism. This fact was borne out when we attended the opening night of *Les Misérables* in Manchester at the Palace Theatre. The champagne flowed and the conversation with fellow performers sparkled. The first half of the show was superb, although the wine I had drunk was making it difficult to focus on the plot. At the interval, we joined several members from the cast of *Coronation Street* in the private bar and my self-punishment began again. I glanced at my watch and saw that the interval was well over the stipulated fifteen minutes – odd, I thought. We took our seats and it was clear that something was up. Thirty minutes had now elapsed and the curtain was still down; one could sense an air of tension in the crowded theatre. I went back to the bar for a refill, then edged my way back again when I saw the glare of disapproval on Tracy's face.

Suddenly the curtain rose and out stepped the man behind the production, Cameron Macintosh himself. 'I'm sorry, ladies and gentlemen,' he said apologetically, 'but the performance cannot continue owing to a fault in the machinery that works the main prop in the production, the stockade scene.... I'm extremely sorry, but the show cannot go on....' There was a deathly silence, then the champagne boosted me from my seat and I shouted down to Macintosh: 'In that case, can you tell us how it ends?' The tension in the theatre was suddenly relieved as the audience exploded into laughter. At the party afterwards, Cameron Macintosh waited for me at the hotel entrance, shook me warmly by the hand and said with a grin: 'Thanks, Les, could you come to all my first nights?'

It was with some trepidation that I went to Victoria Hospital for a video cardiac check-up. Although I was feeling great, my narrow escape from death in London had damaged the valve on the old ticker.... The white-coated and sombre medic ran an instrument all over my chest, sides and back and there on screen was a negative film of my heart. After it was all over, he smiled and said, 'Marvellous, Les, there is a vast improvement.'

My time of recuperation came rapidly to a close and Bournemouth loomed large. The play was greeted with enthusiasm by the holidaymakers and residents alike and the newspaper reviews were quite flattering, in one of them I was referred to as 'That Mancunian Marvel, a portly delight.'

The season trundled along in a sunny and amiable fashion. Tracy and I had rented a house that overlooked the marina in Christchurch. At first we were happy with it but it was a three-storey dwelling and as Tracy's pregnancy inched ahead, going up and down the stairs became an effort of will for her, but for me the stairs and the play plus the nightly trek up the pier, proved that my stamina was still capable of sustaining the gruelling pace of show business.

Tracy and I were wrapped up in each other and our unborn child was the bond. We would drive through the New Forest and drink in the beauty of it all, babbling on about what names we should choose for the baby. We did exactly the same as we rambled along the beach and ditto in the dressing-room.

It was quite the nicest summer season we had spent. The cast of the play – Peter Goodwright, Ron Aldridge, Michael Cotteril, Brian Godfrey, Janet Eddis and Tara Ward, not forgetting our company manager Jon Sowden who doubled as the inept photographer – were a joy to work with, so a big thank you all round.

The hazy early summer ambled by, dappling the blue sea that licked the broad blankets of sand and sent mirrors of warmth bouncing off the white-walled hotels and fine houses of a bygone time.

To me, Bournemouth is a gracious elderly dowager who hasn't quite come to grips with the modern age. I sensed an air of exquisite decay in the resort that was almost a time warp that refused to forget the Edwardian era.

Our happiness knew no bounds and the knowledge of our love growing within Tracy welded us ever closer. The specialist in Bournemouth looked after Tracy with a fatherly eye and all was well as the summer edged into middle August. All of a sudden we experienced weather changes: furious gales humped the sea into small mountains and pelmets of sudden rain hung from darkening skies. Then we received a jolt. During a routine examination, the specialist frowned as he explored Tracy's abdomen ... 'Baby seems small for the length of your pregnancy, my dear, and the heartbeat is faint.'

As he spoke my heart lurched. 'Is it serious doctor?' I managed to stammer. He gave me a shadow of a smile and launched into a maze of medical jargon that I didn't hear: all I could think about was the baby. We left the hospital in a daze. Were we to be robbed of the child we yearned for? We wept quietly.

We moved out of the house in Christchurch and booked into the Royal Bath Hotel for the last ten days of the season. I wanted Tracy, who was looking tired and pale, to have complete rest. She slept and ate well; I made her stay in bed whilst I went to the theatre, and within five days she was looking so much better. She had a scan at the Poole hospital and, much to our relief, the baby had grown.

Home again and it was a delight to wander through our

recently redecorated house. Bournemouth now seemed a hundred years ago as we snuggled close together with me hoping for the baby inside Tracy to kick. The nursery had been completed with the help of our wonderful lady, Jean, who looks after us and the stage was set for the much wanted infant.

Tracy and I have known unhappiness and our love has been forged in adversity and condemnation, but we have emerged from it all with a love so strong it could be likened to steel; now we looked forward to the embodiment of that love....

They say the age of miracles is passed, but on Saturday 3 October 1992 at 2.35 pm in the delivery room at Saint Mary's Maternity Hospital in Manchester I saw such a miracle when I witnessed the slightly premature birth of our daughter, Charlotte Emily Lesley, who struggled into the world a tiny 5lb 6oz to enrich the lives of us both. By doing so she has welded a ring of happiness that will encircle our destiny until the end of time. She arrived fourteen days ahead of schedule and thus gave us an extra fortnight of joy.

This clown will cry no more.

WHEN'S IT COMING OUT?

Maureen Lipman

After the triumphs of *How Was It For You?* and *Something To Fall Back On*, Maureen Lipman's latest confessional is nothing less than the personal and professional equivalent of crazy paving – and guaranteed to have you cracking up.

Since her last bestseller *Thank You For Having Me*, she has skidded down mountains, birdied and bogied – and no doubt beagled – on the golf course, eaten oggies in Cornwall, canard in Cannes and kneidlach in the Catskills. She has survived winged ghosts, topless hosts, A levels, B pictures, hypnosis, psychosis, vacuum salesman overkill and expiring sofas. Oh, and she has been voted 'Columnist of the Year' – and that's just in the daytime. For your evening's entertainment, read how Maureen Lipman put the phone down on Beattie, re-surfaced in *Re: Joyce*, went to the country with *The Cabinet Minister* and was finally found in *Yonkers* – in fact, she's packed in everything but the kitchen shrink. When you finally put this book down, you'll be asking when the next one's coming out!

HOW WAS IT FOR YOU?

Maureen Lipman

In this outrageously funny peep between her loo nets, Maureen Lipman displays the same originality and razor-sharp wit that she brings to her unforgettable characterisations, taking us on an hilarious whirlwind tour of her adventures (and misadventures) on and off stage.

Whether she's frying mints in her ball gown, giving Barbra Streisand tips on her singing, knocking on doors on a freezing February night clad only in a bikini and suntan lotion, having her teeth super-glued, carrying on a vendetta with a megalomaniac cash dispenser or simply hand-rearing a racing tortoise, life with Lipman is predictable only in its hysterical unpredictability . . .

SOMETHING TO FALL BACK ON

Maureen Lipman

Got the blahs? Got the blues? Has life lost all its colour and excitement? Do you feel that all the fun is passing you by? It could be that what you need is . . .

SOMETHING TO FALL BACK ON

Following her first hugely successful foray into print, *How Was It For You?*, Maureen Lipman once again shows us Life with the Lid Off. In this fearless exposé of Muswell Hill mores, she does not flinch from such controversial topics as sex, chimney pots, cucumbers, the Tory Party Chairman, willy-warmers, family planning, cucumbers, bits of fluff, the Watford Gap, sex, bell bottoms, Soho chip shops and cucumbers. Funny? You may never forget her recipe for shampoo-flavored duck soup. But you won't remember when you laughed this much . . .

THANK YOU FOR HAVING ME

Maureen Lipman

Following the triumph of her earlier literary excursions, *How Was It For You?* and *Something To Fall Back On*, Maureen Lipman again examines the warp and weft of her life's particularly rich tapestry.

Coping with tangerine hair and terrified teeth, doing the weekly wash in a floor-length taffeta gown prior to shaking hands with Her Majesty the Queen (with non-biological soap powder under her fingernails), facing the comparative perils of Australian restaurants and English loos with all the quiet composure of a late summer bluebottle – all this is just part of her normal working day.

In between she *About Faces* as wife, mother, elderly British Telecom telephonist, and as the one woman in her one-woman show *Re: Joyce*. Also in her spare time she composes sensitive replies to such appeals as: 'We would like you to do a cabaret at our annual arm-wrestling and spinach risotto evening at The Cock and Pullet in Poplar . . .'

All quite normal really. If you like normality. In which case this is probably not the book for you!

IN FOR A PENNY:

THE UNAUTHORISED BIOGRAPHY OF JEFFREY ARCHER

Jonathan Mantle

Millionaire, bestselling author, ex-MP, successful upholder of a libel action against the tabloid press and ill-fated Tory Deputy Chairman, Jeffrey Archer – now Lord Archer – sounds like a hero of his own fiction. And, to a large extent, that is exactly what he is, as he proceeds into the nineties at his characteristic whirlwind pace; publicity, as ever, his trademark. During the making, unmaking and remaking of his extraordinary career, he has presented to the world a self-styled image of himself. Nobody – until now – has checked the facts behind the fiction.

JACK NICHOLSON

Donald Shepherd

Superstar, sex symbol and hellraiser par excellence, Jack Nicholson is one of the biggest and best-paid stars in Hollywood. Known to millions worldwide through his starring roles in *The Shining*, *Terms of Endearment*, *Prizzi's Honor* and *Batman*, he is equally famed for the 'killer smile' and the dark glasses behind which lurks one of the cinema's most enigmatic personalities.

In this penetrating biography, Donald Shepherd reveals the man behind the public persona, and lifts the lid on his extraordinary background. At the age of thirty-seven, he discovered the reason behind his recurring feeling of rejection: the woman he had believed to be his elder sister was in fact his mother. He had been born illegitimately – a discovery that has had a marked effect on his life and career.

But that career was nearly over by the time he was thirty-two. On the point of abandoning acting, he accidentally wafted to stardom on a marijuana haze with *Easy Rider*. Since then his star has risen to dizzy heights – but his personal life has been chequered. A failed first marriage, a stormy fifteen-year affair with Anjelica Huston, numerous affairs, and now a second marriage have shown that he finds relationships difficult; a problem that has influenced his films and, as the author demonstrates, provoked strange encounters with the likes of James Dean, Marlon Brando and John Belushi.

EYE OF THE TIGER

Frank Bruno

Arguably Britain's most popular sportsman and one of the country's most in-demand personalities, Frank Bruno here tells his own compelling story of his life and career both inside and outside the boxing ring. From the launching-pad of a terraced house in Wandsworth, a tearaway childhood and the Oak Hall school for scoundrels (where he excelled at sport but was forbidden to box), he fought against the odds – and against some of the most famous names in world boxing – to become a major sporting success and a mega public superstar.

Eye of the Tiger reveals his personal hopes and fears when confronting his chief opponents, Joe Bugner and not least Mike Tyson; tells why he carried on boxing after the sort of experiences that would convince most people to hang up their gloves; explains the strange circumstances of his much-publicized break with manager Terry Lawless, and reveals the often painful pressures and prejudices he has had to learn to live with throughout his glittering career.

JOYCE, BY HERSELF AND HER FRIENDS

(ed) *Reggie Grenfell* and *Richard Garnett*

Joyce Grenfell endeared herself to millions by her films, her entertainments and her books. This portrait of Joyce has been compiled by her husband Reggie and by Richard Garnett from the memories of those who knew her and from writings of her own – autobiographical sketches, poems, essays and one or two monologues – that have not been included in her other books.

Those contributing include Joseph Cooper, Richard Baker and Bernard Levin from *Face the Music*, Stephen Potter, Clive James, John Dankworth and Cleo Laine. There are also illustrations from the pen of Sir Hugh Casson.

JOYCE GRENFELL REQUESTS THE PLEASURE

Joyce Grenfell

A legendary entertainer, Joyce Grenfell won the love of millions through her films, her stage and television performances, and her writing. This first volume of her autobiography takes the story from her childhood through the war, to the moment in 1945 when her own show, *Joyce Grenfell Requests the Pleasure*, opened in London.

'*Joyce Grenfell Requests the Pleasure* does for a girlhood in the twenties what books like Gwen Raverat's "Period Piece" or Joan Evans's "Prelude and Fugue" did for an earlier generation. Like those classics of childhood recollection, it is vivid, evocative, bathed in warm clear light and packed with the kind of curious lore one could pick up nowhere else'
Observer

'Read, re-read, laugh and cry over this unique book, but don't lend it to anyone, because if you do you'll never see it again'
Books and Bookmen

'Innumerable merry moments . . . It is to her own contented life that *Joyce Grenfell Requests the Pleasure* of a visit from you and me. Accept the invitation at once'
Sunday Telegraph

'Gripping . . . Joyce Grenfell's brilliant book is a success in the same sense and for the same reasons as are her performances'
The Times